A DOMINIE DISMISSED

This edition published by Lector House in 2024

ISBN: 978-93-6138-362-5

Lector House LLP
Registered Office: H. No. 96, Block C, Tomar Colony,
Burari, Delhi – 110084, India
info@lectorhouse.com
www.lectorhouse.com

A DOMINIE DISMISSED

ALEXANDER SUTHERLAND NEILL

2024

LECTOR HOUSE

LECTOR HOUSE LLP

A DOMINIE DISMISSED

BY

A. S. NEILL

TO THE
ORIGINAL
OF
MARGARET

CONTENTS

Page

1. Chapter I. 1
2. Chapter II. 6
3. Chapter III. 14
4. Chapter IV. 19
5. Chapter V. 30
6. Chapter VI. 36
7. Chapter VII. 43
8. Chapter VIII. 49
9. Chapter IX. 55
10. Chapter X. 62
11. Chapter XI. 68
12. Chapter XII. 73
13. Chapter XIII. 80
14. Chapter XIV. 89
15. Chapter XV. 96
16. Chapter XVI. 102
17. Chapter XVII. 109

A DOMINIE DISMISSED.

CHAPTER I.

I have packed all my belongings. My trunk and two big boxes of books stand in the middle of a floor littered with papers and straw. I had my typewriter carefully packed too, but I took it from out its wrappings, and I sit amidst the ruins of my room with my wee machine before me. It is one of those little folding ones weighing about six pounds.

The London train goes at seven, and it is half-past five now. It was just ten minutes ago that I suddenly resolved to keep a diary . . . only a dominie can keep a Log, and I am a dominie no longer.

I hear Janet Brown's voice outside. She is singing "Keep the Home Fires Burning" . . . and she was in tears this afternoon. The limmer ought to be at home weeping her dominie's departure.

Yet . . . what is Janet doing at my window? Her home is a good two miles along the road. I wonder if she has come to see me off. Yes, she has; I hear her cry to Ellen Smith: "He's packit, Ellen, and Aw hear him addressin' the labels on his typewriter." The besom!

Well, well, children have short memories. When Macdonald enters the room on Monday morning they will forget all about me.

I know Macdonald. He is a decent sort to meet in a house, but in school he is a stern one. His chief drawback is his lack of humour. I could swear that he will whack Jim Jackson for impudence before he is half an hour in the school.

I met Jim one night last week wheeling a box up from the station.

"I say, boy," I called with a pronounced Piccadilly Johnny accent, "heah, boy! Can you direct me to the—er—village post-office?"

He scratched his head and looked round him dubiously.

"Blowed if Aw ken," he said at last. "Aw'm a stranger here."

Yes, Macdonald will whack him.

I sent Jim out yesterday to measure the rainfall (there had been a fortnight's drought) and he went out to the playground. In ten minutes he returned looking puzzled. He came to my desk and lifted an Algebra book, then he went to his seat and seemed to sweat over some huge calculation. At length he came to me and announced that the rainfall was ·3578994 of an inch. I went out to the playground

. . . he had watered it with the watering-can.

"There are no flies on you, my lad," I said.

"No, sir," he smiled, "the flies don't come out in the rain."

Yes, Macdonald is sure to whack him.

I shall miss Jim. I shall miss them all . . . but Jim most of all. What about Janet? And Gladys? And Ellen? And Jean?. . . Well, then, I'll miss Jim most of all the boys.

I tried to avoid being melodramatic to-day. It has been a queer day, an expectant day. They followed me with their eyes all day; if an inspector had arrived I swear that he would have put me down as a good disciplinarian. I never got so much attention from my bairns in my life.

I blew the "Fall in!" for the last time at the three o'clock interval. Janet and Ellen were late. When they arrived they carried a wee parcel each. They came forward to my desk and laid their parcels before me.

"A present from your scholars," said Janet awkwardly. I slowly took off the tissue paper and held up a bonny pipe and a crocodile tobacco-pouch. I didn't feel like speaking, so I took out my old pouch and emptied its contents into the new one; then I filled the new pipe and placed it between my teeth. A wee lassie giggled, but the others looked on in painful silence.

I cleared my throat to speak, but the words refused to come . . . so I lit the pipe.

"That's better," I said with forced cheerfulness, and I puffed away for a little.

"Well, bairns," I began, "I am— —" Then Barbara Watson began to weep. I frowned at Barbara; then I blew my nose. Confound Barbara!

"Bairns," I began again, "I am going away now." Janet's eyes began to look dim, and I had to frown at her very hard; then I had to turn my frown on Jean . . . and Janet, the besom, took advantage of my divided attention. I blew my nose again; then I coughed just to show that I really did have a cold.

"I don't suppose any of you understand why I am going away, but I'll try to tell you. I have been dismissed by your fathers and mothers. I haven't been a good teacher, they say; I have allowed you too much freedom. I have taken you out sketching and fishing and playing; I have let you read what you liked, let you do what you liked. I haven't taught you enough. How many of you know the capital of Bolivia? You see, not one of you knows."

"Please, sir, what is it?" asked Jim Jackson.

"I don't know myself, Jim."

My pipe had gone out and I lit it again.

"Bairns, I don't want to leave you all; you are mine, you know, and the school is ours. You and I made the gardens and rockeries; we dug the pond and we caught the trout and minnows and planted the water-plants. We built the pigeon-loft and the rabbit-hutch. We fed our pets together. We— —"

I don't know what happened after that. I took out my handkerchief, but not to blow my nose.

"The bugle," I managed to say, and someone shoved it into my hand. Then I played "There's No Parade To-day," but I don't think I played it very well.

Only a few went outside; most of them sat and looked at me.

"I must get Jim to save the situation," I said to myself, and I shouted his name.

"P-please, sir," lisped Maggie Clark, "Jim's standin' oot in the porch."

"Tell him to come in," I commanded.

Maggie went out; then she returned slowly.

"P-please, sir, he's standin' greetin' and he winna come."

"Damnation!" I cried, and I bustled them from the room.

A quarter-past six! It's time Jim came for these boxes.

* * * * *

I am back in my old rooms in a small street off Hammersmith Broadway. My landlady, Mrs. Lewis, is a lady of delightful garrulity, and her comments on things to-day have served to cheer me up. She is intensely interested in the fact that I have come from Scotland, and anxious to give me all the news of events that have happened during my sojourn in the wilds.

"Did you 'ear much abaht the war in Scotland?" she said.

I looked my surprise.

"War! What war?"

Then she explained that Britain and France and Russia and the Allies were fighting against Germany.

"Now that I come to think of it," I said reflectively, "I *did* see a lot of khaki about to-day."

"Down't you get the pypers in Scotland?" she asked.

"Thousands of them, Mrs. Lewis; why, every Scot plays the pipes."

"I mean the pypers, not the pypers," she explained.

"Oh, I see! We do get a few; English travellers leave them in the trains, you know."

She thought for a little.

"It must be nice livin' in a plyce w'ere everyone knows everyone else. My sister Sally's married to a pynter in Dundee, Peter Macnab; do you know 'im?"

I explained that Peter and I were almost bosom friends. Then she asked me whether I knew what his wage was. I explained that I did not know. She then told me how much he gave Sally to keep house with, and I began to regret my temerity in claiming a close acquaintance with the erring Peter. Mrs. Lewis at once began to recount the family history of the Macnabs, and I blushed for the company I kept.

I decided to disown Peter.

"Perhaps he'll behave better now that he has gone to Glasgow," I remarked.

"But he ain't gone to Glasgow!" she exclaimed.

I looked thoughtful.

"Ah!" I cried, "I've been thinking of the other Peter Macnab, the painter in Lochee."

"Sally's 'usband lives in a plyce called Magdalen Green."

"Ah! I understand now, Mrs. Lewis. I've met that one too; you're quite right about his character."

If I ever write a book of aphorisms I shall certainly include this one: Never claim an acquaintance with a lady's relations by marriage.

I wandered along Fleet Street to-day, the most fascinating street in London . . . and the most disappointing. To understand Fleet Street you must walk along the Strand at midday. The Londoner is the most childish creature on earth. If a workman opens a drain cap the traffic is held up by the crowds who push forward to glimpse the pipes below. If a black man walks along the Strand half a hundred people will follow him on the off chance that he may be Jack Johnson. London is the most provincial place in Britain. I have eaten cookies in Princes Street in Edinburgh, and I have eaten buns in Piccadilly. The London audience was the greater. Audience! the word derives from the Latin *audio*: I hear. That won't do to describe my eating; spectators is the word.

I wandered about all day, and the interests of the streets kept my thoughts away from that little station in the north. Now it is evening, and my thoughts are free to wander.

A few of them would see Macdonald arrive to-day, and I think that in wondering at him they will have forgotten me. Children live for the hour; their griefs are as ephemeral as their joys, and the ephemeralism of their emotion is as wonderful as its intensity. A boy will bury his brother in the afternoon, and scream at Charlie Chaplin in the evening. He will forget Charlie again, though, when he lies alone in the big double bed at night.

Jim and Janet and Jean and the rest have loved me well, but I have no illusions about their love. Children are painfully docile. In two weeks they will accept Macdonald's iron rule without question, just as they accepted my absence of rule without question. Yet I wonder . . .! Perhaps the love of freedom that I gave them will make them critical now. I know that they gradually developed a keen sense of justice. It was just a fortnight ago that Peter Shaw was reported to me as a slayer of young birds. I formed a jury with Jim Jackson as foreman, and they called for witnesses.

"Gentlemen of the jury, your verdict?" I said.

Jim stood up.

"Accused is acquitted . . . only one witness!"

I used to see them weigh my actions critically, and I had to be very particular not to show any sign of favouritism—a difficult task, for a dominie is bound to like some bairns better than others. Will they apply this method to Macdonald? I rather think he will beat it out of them. He is the type of dominie that stands for Authority with the capital A. His whole bearing shouts: "I am the Law. What I say is right and not to be questioned."

My poor bairns!

CHAPTER II.

I went to Richmond to-day, hired a skiff, and rowed up to Teddington. I tied the painter to a tuft of grass on the bank and lazed in the sunshine. For a time I watched the boats go by, and I smiled at the windmill rowing of a boatload of young Italians. Then a gilded youth went by feathering beautifully . . . and I smiled again, for the Italians seemed to be getting ever so much more fun out of their rowing than this artist got.

By and by the passers-by wearied me, and I thought of my village up north. The kirk would be in. Macdonald would probably be there, and the bairns would be glancing at him sidelong, while I, the failure, lay in a boat among strangers. I began to indulge in the luxury of self-pity; feeling oneself a martyr is not altogether an unpleasant sensation.

I turned my face to the bank and thought of what had taken place. The villagers accused me of wasting their children's time, but when I asked them what they would have me make their children do they were unable to answer clearly.

"Goad!" said Peter Steel the roadman, "a laddie needs to ken hoo to read and write and add up a bit sum."

"Just so," I said. "When you go home to-night just try to help your Jim with his algebra, will you? I'll give you five pounds if you can beat him at arithmetic."

"Aw'm no sayin' that he doesna ken his work," he protested, "but Aw want to ken what's the use o' a' this waste o' time pluckin' flowers and drawin' hooses. You just let the bairns play themsells."

"That's what childhood is for," I explained, "for playing and playing again. In most schools the children work until they tire, and then they play. My system is the reverse; they play until they are tired of play and then they work . . . ask for work."

I know that the villagers will never understand what I was trying to do. My neighbour, Lawson of Rinsley School, had a glimmering of my ideal.

"I see your point," he said, "but the fault of the system is this: you are not preparing these children to meet the difficulties of life. In your school they choose their pet subjects, but in a factory or an office they've got to do work that they may hate. I say that your kids will fail."

"You aren't teaching them character," he added.

Lawson's criticism has made me think hard. I grant that I am not an efficient producer of wage-slaves. The first attribute of a slave is submission; he must never question. Macdonald is the true wage-slave producer. He sets up authority to destroy criticism, and the children naturally accept their later slavery without question. Macdonald is the ideal teacher for the reactionists and the profiteers.

Will my bairns shirk the difficulties of life? There is Dan MacInch. He shirked algebra; he told me frankly that he didn't like it. I said nothing, and I allowed him to read while the others were working algebraical problems. In less than a week he came to me. "Please, sir, give me some algebra for home," he said, and in three weeks he was as good as any of them. I hold that freedom does not encourage the shirking of difficulties. I found that my bairns loved them. Some of them delighted in making them. Jim Jackson would invent the most formidable sums and spend hours trying to solve them.

Of course there were aversions. Jim hated singing and grammar. Why should I force him to take an interest in them? No one forces me to take an interest in card-playing . . . my pet aversion, or in horse-racing.

Freedom allows a child to develop its own personality. If Jim Jackson, after being with me for two years, goes into an office and shirks all unpleasant duties, I hold that Jim is naturally devoid of grit. I allowed him to develop his own personality and if he fails in life his personality is manifestly weak. If Macdonald can turn out a better worker than I can . . . and I deny that there is any evidence that he can . . . I contend that he has done so at the expense of a boy's individuality. He has forced something from without on the boy. That's not education. The word derives from the Latin "to lead forth." Macdonald would have made Jim Jackson a warped youth; he would have Macdonaldised him. I took the other way. I said to myself: "This chap has something bright in him. What is it?" I offered him freedom and he showed me what he was—a good-natured clever laddie with a delightful sense of the comic. I think that his line is humour; more than once have I told him that he has the makings of a great comedian in him. I said this to Lawson and he scoffed.

"Good Lord!" he cried, "what a mission to have in life!"

"Better an excellent Little Tich," I replied, "than an average coal-heaver. To amuse humanity is a great mission, Lawson."

There was wee Doris Slater, the daughter of people who lived in a caravan. That child moved like a goddess. I think that if Pavlova saw Doris she would beg her mother to allow the child to become a dancer. Macdonald would try to make Doris a typist, I fancy, and pride himself on the fact that he had improved her social position. I would have Doris a dancer, for she looks like being fit to become a very great artist. Music moves her to unconscious ecstatic grace in movement.

I want education to guide a child into finding out what best it can do. At present our schools provide for the average child . . . and heaven only knows how many geniuses have been destroyed by stupid coercion. I want education to set out deliberately to catch genius in the bud. And what discovers genius cannot be bad for the children who have no genius.

I want education to produce the best that is in a child. That is the only way to improve the world. The naked truth is that we grown-ups have failed to make the world better than the gigantic slum it is, and when we pretend to know how a child should be brought up we are being merely fatuous. We must hand on what we have learned to the children, but we must do it without comment. We must not say: "This is right," because we don't know what is right: we must not say: "This is wrong," because we don't know what is wrong. The most we should do is to tell a child our experience. When I caught my boys smoking I did not say: "This is wrong"; I merely said: "Doctors say that cigarettes are bad for a boy's health. They are the specialists in health; you and I don't know anything about it."

When I tell a boy that a light should not be taken near to petrol I am handing on bitter experience of my own, but when I say that he must know the chief dates of history by Monday morning I am doing an absolutely defenceless thing, for no one can prove by experience that a knowledge of dates is a good thing. Macdonald would say: "Quite so, but could you prove that it is a bad thing?" I would reply that I could prove it is a senseless thing; moreover education should not aim at giving children things that do not do them harm. I don't suppose that it would do me any harm to learn up the proper names in the Bible beginning with Adam. The point is would it do me any good?

I once had a discussion with Macdonald on Socialism. He accused me of attempting to force humanity to be of a pattern.

"Socialism kills individualism," he said.

I smile to think that the Conservative Macdonald is trying to mould children to a pattern, while I, a Socialist, insist on each child's being allowed to develop its own separate individuality.

The Socialist would appear to be the keenest individualist in the world, for it is from the heretical section of society that the demand for freedom in education is coming.

* * * * *

To-day I visited Watterson, an old college friend of mine. He is now in Harley Street, and is fast becoming famous as a specialist in nervous disorders.

"Your nerves are all to pot," he said; "what have you been doing with yourself?"

I told him my recent history.

"But, Good Lord!" he cried, "how did you manage to find any worry in a village?"

I tried to explain. Living in a village narrows one; the outside world is gradually forgotten, and the opinions of ignoramuses gradually come to matter. I found myself beginning to worry over the adverse criticisms of villagers who could not read nor write.

"You've got neurasthenia," said Watterson; "what you want to do is to settle down on a farm for six months; live in the open air and do nothing strenuous. Don't try to think, and for God's sake don't worry. Read *John Bull* and *The Pink 'Un*, and chuck all the weekly intellectual reviews. And . . . most important of all, fall in love with a rosy-cheeked daughter of the soil."

I have written to Frank Thomson, the farmer of Eagleshowe, asking if he still wants a cattleman. His last man was conscripted, and if the job is still vacant Frank will give it to me.

To-night I sit chuckling. The idea of a dismissed dominie's returning to a village to feed cattle is rich. The village will extract much amusement out of it. I imagine Peter Mitchell looking over the dyke and crying: "Weel, dominie, and how is the experiment in eddication gettin' on?"

* * * * *

I sit at a bright peat fire in Frank Thomson's bothy. I arrived at three o'clock and no bairn was about the station. I was glad, for I did not want to meet anyone. There was a queer feeling of shame in returning; I feared to meet anyone's glance. To return a few days after an affecting farewell is the last word in anticlimax; it is so horribly undramatic a thing to do. I wish that Lazarus had kept a diary after his resurrection; I fancy that quite a few people resented his return.

I cannot write more to-night; I am tired out. The most tiring thing in the world is to rise in one place and go to bed in another.

* * * * *

I was going out to fetch the cows this afternoon when I espied three girls in white pinafores at the top of the field. They waved their hands and ran down to meet me.

"We'll help you to take in the cows," cried Janet. They accepted my return without even the slightest curiosity, and I was glad.

"Righto!" I said, "but wait a bit. I want to sketch the farm first."

I sat down on the bank and the three settled themselves round me.

"Please, sir," said Ellen, "Mr. Macdonald's a nice man."

I did not want to discuss Macdonald with my bairns, and I sketched in silence. I think they forgot all about my presence after that; in the old days they used to talk to each other as if I weren't there. Once they discussed likely sweethearts in the village for me, and I am sure they forgot that I was there.

"He's nice to the lassies, Ellen," said Jean, "but not to the boys."

"What did he strap Jim Jackson for?" asked Ellen.

"Aw dinna ken," said Janet, "but he was needin' the strap. Jim Jackson's a cheeky wee thing."

"Eh!" said Jean, "haven't we to sit awful quiet, Jan?"

"Weel," said Janet nodding her head sagely, "and so ye shud sit quiet in the schule. Ye'll no be learning yer lessons if ye speak."

I went on sketching.

Janet is already being Macdonaldised. She accepts his authority without question. Ellen and Jean are critical as yet, but in a week both will have adapted themselves to the machine.

They wandered off to pluck flowers. I finished my sketch and hailed them. Then they came to me and took my arms and we took the cows home.

In the evening I was mucking out the byre when Jim Jackson came for his milk.

"Good morrow, sir," I called from the byre door, "you didn't happen to see Mr. Thomson's elephant as you came up the road?"

He looked interested.

"Elephant?" he asked brightly.

"Yes. The white one; strayed away this afternoon from the chicken coop. Have you seen it?"

"No," he said, "not the white one, but the grey one and the tiger are sitting at the dyke-side down at the second gate. I gave the tiger a turnip when I passed it."

"Good!" I cried, "always be kind to animals."

"Yes, sir," he said, and he glanced down to the second gate. I think that he wouldn't have been very much surprised if he had seen a tiger there. Jim has the power of make-believe developed strongly. A few weeks ago he found a dead sparrow in the playground. He came to me and asked for a coffin. I gave him a match-box and he lined the class up in twos and led them with bared heads towards the grave he had dug. The four foremost boys carried the coffin shoulder high.

Jim laid ropes over the grave and the coffin was lowered reverently. A boy was just about to fill in the grave when Jim cried: "Hold on!" Then he took a handful of earth and sprinkled it over the coffin saying: "Dust to dust, and ashes to ashes."

I blew the Last Post over the grave afterwards. Jim was as serious as could be; for the moment he seemed to think that he was burying his brother.

When he had got his milk he came to the byre door and watched me work for a little.

"Please, sir," he asked, "do you like that better than teaching?"

I told him that I didn't.

"I wish Mester Macdonald wud be a cattleman," he said fervently.

"Some folk might say that he is," I remarked.

"He gave me my licks the first mornin' he cam," he continued. "We got an essay 'How I spent my holidays,' and I said that I was in France and helped the Crown Prince to loot places. We quarrelled about how much we should get each and I shot him. The Mester gave me three scuds for tellin' lies."

"He would," I said grimly.

"But you used to tell me to tell lies!" he cried.

"I did, Jim. And you see the result. . . . I muck out a byre."

When Jim went away I came to a sudden resolution: I would fight for Jim. I'll do all in my power to help the lad to preserve his own personality. . . . Frank Thomson is his uncle and I'll try to get Jim to see me often. Professional etiquette! Professional etiquette be damned! I'm not in the profession now anyhow, and all the professional etiquette in the world is as nothing to the saving of a soul.

* * * * *

I find that I enjoy my food now. Formerly I looked on a meal as an appetiser for a smoke; now I look on a meal as an event. I feel healthier than I ever did in my life before. The land dulls one, however. The old cry "Back to the Land" means "Back to Elemental Mental Stagnation." I spent this forenoon cutting turnips, and I know that I thought of nothing all the time. I have a theory that great thoughts are the product of disease. Possibly this is only another way of saying that genius is allied to madness. Shelley was a physical weakling; Ibsen and Nietzsche went mad. Yes, geniuses are diseased folk, but the converse does not hold.

Macdonald came up to see me to-night; he wanted to ask a few things about the school. We lay on a bank and lit our pipes.

"I can't find your 'Record of Work,'" he said.

"I never kept one."

"But . . . the Code demands one!"

"I know . . . but I didn't keep one. My record of work is my pupils in after life."

"Yes," he said drily, "I know all about that, but you are supposed to keep a record that will show an inspector what you are doing to produce this after life record."

"Macdonald," I said impatiently, "if you mean to tell me that any man can tell what I am doing to prepare children for after life by squinting at a crowd of entries of the Took-the-History-of-the-Great-Rebellion-this-week order . . . well, I don't understand your attitude to life in general."

"That's all very well," he protested, "but we aren't there to make the rules; we're paid servants who have to administer the laws of wiser men."

"How do you know that they are wiser?" I asked.

"They're wiser than I am anyway," he said with a smile.

"I'm not so sure of it, Macdonald; they are more unscrupulous than you are. They know what they want, definitely and finally; they want efficient wage-slaves."

"That's merely a Socialistic cry."

"It may be, but it's true. Who rule us? A definite governing class of trained aristocrats."

"H'm! I shouldn't call Lloyd George and that Labour man Hodge trained aristocrats."

"They aren't born aristocrats I admit, but they are aristocratised democrats. They've adapted themselves to the aristocratic tradition. They are on the side of aristocracy; you won't find them alienating the good opinion of the moneyed classes. We are governed from above; do you admit that?"

"In the main . . . yes," he said grudgingly.

"Very good! Well, then, our rulers believe in two kinds of education. They send their sons to the public schools where boys are trained to be governors, but they send the rest of the sons of the community to State schools where they are trained to be disciplined and content with their lot."

"That's nonsense."

"Possibly, but I suppose you know that the members of the House of Lords and the Cabinet don't send their sons to L.C.C. schools."

"You are simply preaching class war," he said.

"I am. There is a class war—there has been for generations—but it is a one-sided war."

"It is," said Macdonald grimly.

"The upper class took the offensive long ago, and it keeps it yet. Look at the squire down in the village. He won't ride in the same railway compartment with you or me; he won't sit beside us in the theatre . . . why, he won't lie beside us in the kirkyard: he's got that railed-off corner for his family. I don't blame him; he has been educated up in his belief, just as you and I have been educated up in the belief that we are his inferiors. When I was down in the school I lectured the whole class one day because I saw a boy doff his cap to the squire and nod to his mother three seconds afterwards.

"Don't you see that this village is a little British Empire? Here there are only two classes—the big house and the village . . . the ruling class and the ruled. The school trains the ruled to be ruled, and the kirk takes up the training on the Seventh Day. The minister talks a lot of prosy platitudes about Faith and Love and Charity, but he never thinks of saying a thing that the squire might take umbrage at."

I broke off and refilled my pipe.

"How are you getting on?" I asked.

"Well enough. The bairns are nice."

"A little bit noisy," he added, "but, of course, I was prepared for that. I heard about your experiment months ago. By the way, what sort of a teacher is Miss Watson?"

"Excellent," I replied.

"How often did you examine her classes?"

"I never examined her classes, not formally, but her bairns spoke to me, and I judged her work from their conversation."

"I examined their work yesterday; her spelling is weak and her geography atrocious."

"Shouldn't wonder," I said carelessly. "I never bothered about those things; I judged her work by what her bairns were, not by what they knew. They're a bright lot when you ask them to think out things."

"No wonder they fired you out," he laughed; "you're impossible as a dominie, you know."

I smiled.

"How do you like Jim Jackson?" I asked suddenly.

"Cheeky devil!"

"He's clever," I said.

"You may call it cleverness, but I have another name for it. He is a fellow that requires to be sat on."

"And you'll sit on him?"

"I certainly shall . . . heavily too."

I tried to show Macdonald that he was making a criminal blunder, but he got impatient. "I can't stand cheek," he kept saying, and I had to give up all hope of convincing him that I was right. Macdonald is essentially a stupid man. I don't say that merely because he disagrees with me; I say it because he refuses to think out his own attitude. He cries that Jim is cheeky, but he won't go into the other question as to whether humour is impudence. Had he argued that humour is a drawback in life I should have pitied his taste, but I should have admired his ability to make out a good case.

CHAPTER III.

I have spent a hard day forking hay along with Margaret Thomson. Margaret is twenty and bonny, but she is very, very shy. She attended my Evening class last winter, and she appears to be afraid to speak to me. I tried to get her to converse again and again to-day, but it was of no use. I think that she fears to make a mistake in grammar or to mispronounce a word.

I hear her voice outside at the horse-trough. She is bantering old Peter Wilson, and talking thirteen to the dozen. Her laugh is a most delightful thing. I wonder did Touchstone like Audrey's laugh!

The Thomsons are carrying out in farming the principles I set myself to carry out in education. They treat their beasts with the greatest kindness. There isn't a wild animal in the place. Spot the collie is a most lovable creature; the sheep are all tame, and the cows are quiet beasts; the bull has a bold eye, but he is as gentle as a lamb. The horses come to the kitchen door from the water-trough, and little Nancy Thomson feeds them with bread. Every member of the family comes into personal immediate contact with the animals, and the animals seem to love the family. There is no fear in this farmyard.

Mrs. Thomson is a kind-hearted soul. She never goes down to the village unless to the kirk on Sunday. She works hard all day, but she is always cheerful. "I like to see them comin' in aboot," she says, and she seems to find the greatest pleasure in preparing the family's meals. On a Saturday bairns come up from the village, and she gives them "pieces" spread thick with fresh butter and strawberry jam. "I'm never happy unless there's a squad o' bairns roond me," she said to me to-day.

Frank Thomson is what the village would call a funny sort o' a billie. His eyes are always twinkling, and he tries to see the funny side of life. He hasn't much humour, but he has a strong sense of fun, and he loves to chaff the youngsters.

"Weel, Wullie," is his invariable greeting when his boy returns from school in the evening, "Weel, Wullie, and did ye get yer licks the day?"

On a Saturday Frank always has a troop of girls hanging on to his coat tails, and he is always playing practical jokes on them—locking them in the stable or covering them with straw.

"Goad!" he will cry, "ye're an awfu' pack o' tormentors; just wait er Aw tell the dominie aboot ye!" and they yell at him.

Mrs. Thomson tells me that he is inordinately proud of having me for a cattleman, and at the cattle mart he boasts about having an M.A. as feeder. I took two stots into the mart yesterday, and when they entered the ring a wag cried: "Are they weel up in the Greek, think ye, Frank?" and the farmers roared.

"Oh, aye," shouted Frank, "they're weel crammed up wi' a'thing that's guid!"

I think that the Scotch Education Department should insist on every teacher's going farming every three years. Inside the profession you lose perspective. The educational papers are full of articles about geography and history and drawing, but teachers seldom show that they are looking beyond the mere curriculum. The training colleges supply the young teacher with what they call Mental Philosophy or Psychology, but it is quite possible for an honours graduate in mental philosophy to have no philosophy at all.

The question for the teacher is: What am I aiming at? Macdonald is aiming at what he calls a bright show before the inspector. To be just to the man I admit that he is honestly trying to educate these bairns according to his lights. He wants to produce good scholars, but when I ask him what he considers the goal of humanity he is at sea.

He tells me that education should not be made to produce little Socialists as I seemed to try to do. But I deny that I ever tried to make my bairns Socialists. I told them the elemental truth that a parasite is an enemy of society; I told them that the world was out of joint. And I gave them freedom to develop their personalities in the hope that, freed from discipline and fear and lies, they might become a better generation than mine has been.

The Macdonalds of life have failed to produce thinking that is free; I merely say: Let the children have a say now; stop thrusting your stupid barbaric Authority down their little throats; let the bairns be free to breathe. Give up all the snobbish nonsense about manners and respect and servility you ram into the child; if he refuses to lift his hat to you, who the devil are you that you should coerce him into doing it?

I think that some of the more important villagers were annoyed at the bairns' obvious lack of respect, or at least the semblance of respect. But they looked for faults. They told me of escapades after school hours, of complaints of bosses against boys who had been with me. I asked George Wilson, the mason, whether he would expand his criticism to include the minister. "Do you blame Mr. Gordon for every drunk and every theft in the village? He has been here for thirty years, and, on your reasoning, he has been a failure."

"Aw dinna pay rates for keepin' up the kirk," he replied, "but I pay rates to keep up the schule, and Aw have a claim to creeticise the wye ye teach the bairns."

I see now that I never had a chance against the enemy. They could point to what they called faults . . . Johnnie didn't know his History, Lizzie did too much sketching, Peter wasn't deferential. I could point to nothing. I had abolished fear, I had made the school a place of joy, I had encouraged each child's natural bent . . . and the village smiled scornfully and said: "We ken nae difference."

I found myself worrying over the opinions of small men who are of no importance in the world of ideas; stupid fools led me into taking up an eternal position of defence. And I fumed inwardly, for I am not always a ready talker.

But now I am able to smile at the men who baited me a few weeks ago. They don't count. In the great world beyond the hills there are people who take the large broad view of education, and some day education will really be a "leading forth" not a "putting in."

* * * * *

I met Macdonald to-night, and I asked him how things were doing.

"I'm in the middle of prizes," he said wearily, "and if there's one thing I detest it's prizes."

I began to think that I had misjudged Macdonald.

"Excellent!" I cried, "we agree for once! What's your objection to prizes?"

"They're such a confounded nuisance."

"Granted," I said.

"That's all I have against them. You never know how you are to distribute the things."

"Why do you object to them?" he asked.

I sat down on Wilkie's dyke and lit my pipe.

"I object to them on principle, Macdonald. They're tips, that's what they are."

"Tips?"

"Yes. I give a porter tuppence for seeing my bicycle into the van; I give Mary Ritchie a book for beating the others at reading. I tip both."

"I don't see it."

"The porter shouldn't get a tip; his job is to look after luggage. Mary's job is to read to improve her mind."

"But," said Macdonald, "life is full of rewards."

"I know." Here Peter Mitchell strolled up. "We're talking about prizes," I explained. "Life is full of rewards of all kinds, but the only reward that matters is the joy in doing a thing well. If I write a poem or paint a picture I'm not writing or painting with one eye on royalties or the auction room. I sell my poem or picture in order to live . . . in a decent civilisation I wouldn't require to sell it to live, but that's by the way. My point is that prizes are artificial rewards, just as strapping is an artificial punishment."

"Goad!" said Peter Mitchell, "do ye mean to tell me that Aw wasna thinkin' o' the reward when I selt my powney last Saturday?"

"Competition is a good thing," said Macdonald. "Look at running and sports and all that sort of thing."

"I admit it," I said, "you like to beat your partner at golf. But my contention is that the prize at the end is vulgar; the joy is in being the best sprinter in the country. After all you don't glory in the fact that Simpson took seven at the tenth hole;

your glory lies in the thought that you did it in three.

"Prizes in school are not only vulgar: they are cruel. Take Ellen Smith. Ellen has always been a first-rate arithmetician; she has the talent. For the past four years she has carried off the first prize for arithmetic. Sarah Nelson is very good, but work as she likes she can't beat Ellen. Sarah becomes despondent every year at prize-giving time. Bairns aren't philosophical; they don't see that the vulgar little book they get isn't worth thinking about. The ignorant noodles who sit on School Boards (Peter Mitchell had moved on by this time) stand up at the school exhibition and talk much cant about prizes. 'Them that don't get them this year must just make a spurt and get them next year.' And the poor bairns imagine that a prize is the golden fruit of life."

I notice that the men who are keenest on school prizes are firm believers in school punishments. And they are generally religious. Their god is a petty tyrant who rewards the good and punishes the wicked. They try to act up to the attitude of their god . . . hence, I fancy the term "tin god."

* * * * *

I see that many eminent people are making speeches about "Education After the War." I can detect but little difference between their attitude and that of the commercial men who keep shouting "Capture Germany's Trade!" "Let us have more technical instruction," cries the educationist, "more discipline; let us beat Germany at her own game!" The commercial man chuckles. "Excellent!" he cries, "first-rate . . . but of course we must have Protection also!"

And the educationist and the commercial man will have their way. Education will aim frankly at turning out highly efficient wage-slaves. The New Education has commenced; its first act was to abolish freedom. Free speech is dead; a free press is merely a name; the workers were wheedled into giving up their freedom to sell their commodity labour to the highest bidder, while the profiteer retains his right to sell his goods at the highest price he can get. Every restriction on liberty is alleged to be necessary to win the war.

The alarming feature of the present Prussianisation of Britain lies in the circumstance that the signing of peace will be but the beginning of a new war. If the plans of the Paris Economic Conference are carried out true education is interned for a century. Millions have lost their lives in the military war: millions will lose their souls in the trade war. Just as we have sullenly obeyed the dictates of the war government, we shall sullenly obey the dictates of the trade government. "We must win the trade war," our rulers will cry, and, if the profiteers say that men must work sixteen hours a day if we are to beat Germany, the Press and the Church and the School will persuade the public that the man who strikes for a fifteen hours day is a traitor to his country.

Will anyone try to save education? The commercial men will use it to further their own plans; the educationists will unconsciously play into the profiteers' hands; the women . . . only the other day the suffrage band was marching through the streets of London displaying a huge banner bearing the words "We Want Hughes." Hughes is the Premier of Australia, a Labour man dear to the hearts of all the capitalist newspapers. His one text is "Trade after the War."

Who is there to save education? The teaching profession could save it, but teachers are merely servants. They will continue to argue about Compulsory Greek and, no doubt, Compulsory Russian will come up for discussion in the educational papers soon. The commercially-minded gentlemen of Westminster will draw up the new scheme of education, and the teachers will humbly adapt themselves to the new method.

I don't think that anyone will save education.

CHAPTER IV.

I lay on a bank this afternoon smoking. Janet and Jean and Annie came along the road, and they sat down beside me.

"I'm tired of the school," said Annie wearily; "Aw wish Aw was fourteen!"

"What's wrong now?" I asked.

"Oh, we never get any fun now, the new mester's always so strict, and we get an awful lot o' home lessons now."

"Annie got the strap on Friday," explained Jean. "Mester Macdonald's braces broke Aw think, at least something broke when he was bending doon and he took an awful red face . . . and he had to keep his hands in his pouches till night time to keep his breeks up."

"Did Annie pull them down?" I asked.

Jean tittered.

"No, but she laughed and he gave her the strap."

"Aye," cried Annie in delight, "and they nearly cam doon when he was strap-pin' me!"

"Why do awkward incidents occur to dignity?" I said, more to myself than to the bairns, "my braces wouldn't break in fifty years of teaching." Then I laughed.

Margaret Thomson came down the road on her way to Evening Service, and she reddened as she passed.

"Eh!" laughed Janet, looking up into my face, "did ye see yon? Maggie blushed! Aw wudna wonder if she has a notion o' the Mester!"

"How could she help it, Jan?" I said. "Why, you'll be hopelessly in love with me yourself in a couple of years, you besom!"

She stared before her vacantly for a little.

"Aw did have a notion o' you when ye cam first," she said slowly.

I put my arm round her neck.

"You dear kid!" I said.

She smiled up in my face.

"Ye had that bonny striped tie on then," she said artlessly.

I pulled her hair.

"Ye shud marry Maggie Tamson," she said after a pause.

"Aye," added Jean, "and syne ye'll get the farm when her father dies. He's troubled wi' the rheumatics and he'll no live very long. And she wud be a gran worker too."

"Dinna haver, Jean," said Annie scornfully, "the Mester will want a gran lady for his wife, one that can play the piano and have ham and egg to her breakfast ilka morning."

"No extravagant wife like that for me!" I protested.

"Aweel, an egg ilka day and ham and egg on Sundays onywye," compromised Annie.

"An egg every second morning, Annie," I said firmly, "and ham and egg every second Sunday."

"Ladies dinna mak good wives," said Janet. "Willie Macintosh along at Rinsley married a lassie that was a piano teacher, and she gets her breakfast in her bed and has a wumman to wash up. Aye, and she's ay dressed and oot after dinner-time. Aye, and she sends a' his collars to the laundry . . . and he only wears a clean dicky on Sawbath."

"Ah!" I said, "I'm glad you told me that, Janet; I won't risk marrying a lady. But tell me, Janet, how am I to know what sort of woman I am marrying?"

"It's quite easy," she said slowly, "you just have to tear a button off your waist-coat and if she doesna offer to mend it ye shouldna tak her."

"And speer at her what time she gets up in the mornin'," she added; "Maggie Tamson rises at five ilka mornin'."

"Why are you so anxious that it should be Margaret?" I asked with real curiosity.

Janet shook her head.

"Aw just think she's in love wi' ye," she said simply; "she blushed."

* * * * *

I went out with my bugle to-night, and I sounded all the old calls. I finished up with "Come for Orders," and I walked slowly down the brae to the farm. Jim Jackson and Dickie Gibson came running up to me.

"Ye played 'Come for Orders!'" panted Jim as he wiped his sweating face with his bonnet.

"We'll soon remedy matters," I laughed, and I played the "Dismiss."

Jim perched himself on a gate.

"We'll hae to fall oot, Dick," he said with mock resignation, "come on and we'll sit here till we get oor wind back." And Dick climbed up beside him.

"How are the lies getting on, Jim?" I asked.

He shook his head dolefully.

"We got an essay the day on The Discovery of America . . . and ye canna tell mony lies aboot that. Aw just said that Columbus discovered America, and wrote aboot his ships. The new Mester says we must stick to the truth."

"It is difficult to associate the truth with America," I said. "But there is a true side to this discovery business. To say that Columbus discovered America is a half-truth; the whole truth is that America isn't quite discovered yet. Andrew Carnegie was fairly successful, and Charlie Chaplin is another discoverer of note, but—"

Jim clearly did not understand; he thought that I was pulling his leg.

"How's the pond?" I asked, and was grieved to find that neither of the boys had any interest in it. "The Mester taks us oot and gies us object lessons on the minnows," said Dickie, and I groaned.

"And the pigeons?"

"Object lessons too," said Jim with evident disgust. "What family did he say doos belonged to, Dick?"

Dick had no idea.

"The word dove comes from the Latin *columba,*" I said sententiously. "Hence the name Columbus who was named after the dove that was sent out of the Ark. When he learned this as a boy he resolved to live up to his name . . . hence the American Eagle, which of course has transformed itself into a dove during Woodrow Wilson's reign."

Dick listened open-mouthed, but Jim's eyes twinkled.

"The Mester gives us derivations ilka day. He telt us the derivation of pond when he was giein' us the object lesson, but I canna mind what it was."

"A weight!" cried Dickie suddenly, and I complimented him on his industry.

"Aye," giggled Jim, "he *shud* mind it, for he had to write it oot a hunder times."

I made a cryptic remark about ponds and ponderosity, and then I told them of the boy who had to stay in and write the phrase "I have gone" many times in order that he might grasp the correct idiom. He filled five pages; then he wrote something at the bottom of the last page, a message to his teacher. The message read "Please, sir, I have went home." Dickie immediately asked whether the boy got a lamming next morning, and Jim looked at him scornfully. Dickie has not got an alert mind.

To-night I am doubting whether I was wise to return to the village. I seem to become sadder every day. My heart is down in the old ugly school, and I am jealous of Macdonald. I know that he is an inferior, but he has my bairns in his control. I confess to a sneaking delight in the knowledge that he is not liked by the bairns. In this respect I think I am inferior to him; I don't think he is jealous of my popularity but of course he may be after all.

Jim's answering my bugle call makes me want to cry. I can sit out the most pathetic drama unemotionally; when the hero says farewell for ever to the heroine I sit up cheerfully. It is sweetness that affects me; when the hero clasps his love in his arms I snivel. In the cinema when little Willie is dying to slow music and the mother is wringing her hands I smile, but if Willie recovers and sits up in bed to hug his teddy bear I blow my nose. I am unaffected when Peter Pan returns to find his mother's window shut against him, but when the fairies build a house over the sleeping lost girl I have to light my pipe and cough sternly.

I wish I hadn't gone out with my bugle to-night.

* * * * *

Macdonald is an ass. He came to me this afternoon. "Look here," he began, "I wonder if you've any objection to my making a few alterations in the school live stock?"

"Want to introduce a cow?" I asked. "You believe in utilitarianism in education I fancy."

"It's the pigeons and rabbits," he went on; "I was wondering if you would object to my getting rid of one or two."

"What's wrong?"

"It's the sex matter," he said hurriedly. "I don't like the thing; I don't so much mind the infants asking awkward questions, but why the deuce should they keep them till I am speaking to the infant mistress?"

"Refer them to the lady," I said with a chuckle.

He looked troubled.

"I must get rid of one sex," he said.

"Macdonald," I said severely, "I don't know that you can do that without the permission of the children. The rabbits and doos are their's; they bought them with their own money."

"That's no great difficulty," he said lightly.

"Possibly not . . . not for you, Macdonald. If you use authority the bairns will hardly question it. But I don't see that you have the right to be an autocrat in this affair."

"It is my duty to protect the children," he said with dignity.

"Protect yourself, you mean!" I cried; "you have just confessed that your one aim is to get rid of awkward questions."

"But what can I do?" he stammered.

"Do! Do nothing, just as I did. Let the creatures breed as much as they darned well please; that's what they are there for. You can't very well make sex an object lesson; the logical thing to do is to give a lesson on pollination of plants and then go on to fertilisation of the bird's egg, but if you do that you'll get the sack at once. But there's quite enough of prudery in the world already without your turning a rabbit-hutch into a sultanless harem."

"There are things that children shouldn't know," he said with a touch of aggression.

"And there are things that grown-ups should know and don't," I said. "They ought to know that the sex conspiracy of silence is idiotic and criminal."

"Anyway," he said sullenly, "I'll tell them to-morrow that there are too many in the house and that I mean to get rid of a few."

"All right," I said resignedly, "you can lie to them if you want to." Then I added: "Although, mind you, Macdonald, I feel like telling the bairns the real reason for your action."

He looked startled.

"Don't be alarmed," I said with a smile, "I won't do it," and he looked relieved.

"Why not look in at the school some afternoon?" he said amiably when we parted, "but perhaps you feel that you've shaken off the dust from your feet down there?"

"I'll be delighted to come down," I said; "I didn't shake off the dust from my feet when I left . . . there was quite enough dust there already."

I think I'll go down to-morrow afternoon; it was decent of Macdonald to ask me after all that I have said to him.

* * * * *

A man spends his life wishing he had done certain things and wishing that he had not done certain things. I half wish that I had not accepted Macdonald's invitation; I feel lonely up here now: on the other hand I am glad that I went. I think now that Macdonald's real idea was to show me how he has improved the school.

From his point of view he has improved it. He showed me exercise books that were models of neatness and care; he showed me classes swotting up subjects laboriously; the rooms were as silent as the grave.

When I went in Macdonald shook hands with me formally, and I noticed that his school voice and manner were prim and professional. I turned to the bairns and said: "Hullo, kids!" and they rose in a body and said: "Good afternoon, sir!"

"Ah!" I whispered to Macdonald, "I see I ought to have said: 'Good afternoon, children!' eh?" and he smiled professionally.

The higher classes were drawing. The model was a vase. I walked round the class . . . and swore silently. I had spent two years persuading these bairns that there is no boundary line in nature; a white vase appears to have lines as boundaries simply because it usually stands in front of a dark background. I made them work in the background to show up the model, although I never gave them vases or pails; my drawing was all outside sketching of trees and houses. He was making them "line in" the drawing.

"I am not much good at drawing," he explained apologetically, "as a matter of fact I know nothing about it."

"In that case," I said, "why not let them go on with the methods I gave them? I know something about the subject."

He asked what my methods were and I explained them in a few minutes. He expressed his gratitude and seemed honestly glad to learn something about the subject.

"I won't take them out drawing though," he said; "an inspector might come to the school in my absence."

"You conscientious devil!" I said, "let's have a squint at their exercise books."

As he moved to the cupboard a boy whispered to his neighbour and Macdonald turned like a flash; the lad visibly quailed before his fixing eye. I fancied that the next inspector's report would commence with the words: "The discipline of this school is excellent."

The books were much neater than mine had been. I began to look for blots, but the search was hopeless.

"Oh! for God's sake, Macdonald, show me Peter Mackay's book; surely a good healthy blot will be found there!" But Peter's book was scrupulously clean.

"I had to deal with that boy with a stern hand," said Macdonald grimly, and as I stood looking at the book I saddened.

"On the outside of this book you should write the words: 'Peter Mackay . . . a Tragedy, by William Macdonald,'" I said, but I don't think the man understood me.

The three o'clock interval came. "Stand!" commanded Macdonald, and the class rose as one child. "Front seat . . . quick march!" The boys saluted him as they passed out, and the girls curtsied. I tried not to laugh at the fatuous fellow's inculcation of "respect." Poor devil, I think they will hate him in after years; he is of the brand of dominie that is responsible for the post-schooldays habit of shying divots and opprobrious epithets at teachers passing along the road.

On the way out Janet touched my arm playfully, but the eagle-eyed disciplinarian saw the action and he glared at her.

"Had you any trouble with swearing?" he asked when the last boy had gone out.

"Not particularly. Have you?"

"I've put it down with a very firm hand."

"I never bothered about it," I said carelessly. "I very seldom heard it; if I did happen to hear a boy string together a few strong words I ridiculed him, told him they didn't mean anything. Once I was trying to unscrew a stiff nut from my motor-bike and I addressed it audibly. I heard a snigger and on looking round found that Jim Jackson had come up to watch my efforts."

Macdonald raised his eyebrows and whistled.

"Pretty awkward, eh?"

"Not in the least, Macdonald; I merely said: 'Jim, never waste good bad language; one day you may be a motor-cyclist and you'll need it all then.' Jim nodded approvingly."

"You would have persuaded Jim that he never heard your words," I added.

I find that I cannot dislike Macdonald. He is essentially a decent fellow with a kindly nature; sometimes I feel that I am quite fond of him. His equanimity is charming; he seldom shows the least trace of irritation when I talk to him. But his mental laziness riles me; he is so cock-sure about his methods of education, and I know that I never can induce him to think the matter out for himself. The tragedy is that there are a thousand Macdonalds in Scots schools to-day. Of course they are hopelessly wrong. I don't know whether I am right, but I know that they are wrong. They stick to a narrow code; they force youth to follow their silly behests regarding respect; they kill the individuality of each child. Why in all the earth does civilisation allow such asses to warp the children? Who is Macdonald that any human being should quail before his awful eye? Is he so righteous that he shall punish a boy for swearing? He spent a whole morning lately cross-examining the bairns to discover who wrote the words: "Mr. Macdonald is daft" on the pigeon-house door. At last one wee chap was intimidated into confessing, and Macdonald whacked him and then harangued the whole school. The bairns were convinced that the lad had committed the sin against the Holy Ghost.

What a mind the man has! I discovered an obscene writing about myself three weeks after I had come to the school. The bairns held their breath while I read it. I sent for a cloth and erased the words.

"What's the use of scribbling silly rot like that?" I said, and lit my pipe. There never was any more writing on the wall in my time.

How the devil are bairns to gain any perspective in life if a fool like Macdonald spends half a day investigating nothing? Education should aim at giving a child a philosophy, and philosophy simply means the contemplation of the important things in life. If teachers emphasise the importance of things like silence and manners and dignity and respect, we cannot expect our children to rise higher in later years than the cheap gossipy lying press and the absurd system we call party politics.

The Macdonalds start out with the assumption that human nature is bad; I start out with the realisation that human nature is good. That is the real distinction between the disciplinarian and the believer in freedom. When my boys stole turnips, wrote swear words on walls, talked and ate sweets as they sat in class I attached little or no importance to their actions; all I tried to do was to bring out the best that was in a lad's nature . . . and I succeeded. Every child improved . . . no, I was forgetting one boy! He came from a city school, and his face was full of impudence. He looked round my free school and marvelled; he had come from a Macdonaldised school and he naturally concluded that I was a soft mark. One day I said to him very mildly: "My gentle youth, this school is Liberty Hall, not because I am weak but because I happen to be rather strong. . . . I could whack you effectively if I started to you." But I never managed to fit that boy into my scheme of things. He left after a few months, and after he had gone he bounced to other boys that he had shoved many pens and ink-pots down a hole in the floor. I found that he was telling the truth.

What would have happened if the boy had remained at school I don't know, but I think that he would have gradually adapted himself to his environment. He had been reared in the schools where physical force reigned, and he understood no other system. Yes, I fancy I could have converted that youth. I think of Homer T. Lane and his Little Commonwealth in Dorset, where so called criminal children from the police courts are given self-government and become excellent citizens, and I know that the Macdonalds are wrong.

Not long ago Edinburgh School Board passed a motion asking the local magistrates to make their birch-rod sentences severe enough to be effective. Once upon a time people thought that lunatics were criminals and they lashed them with whips. A time came when people realised that a lunatic was a diseased person and they at once began to care for him tenderly. Nowadays the enlightened members of society realise that a criminal is a diseased person . . . usually the victim of a diseased society . . . and they passionately advocate his being treated as a sick man is treated. And the School Board of the capital of Scotland recommend that extra stripes with the rod be given to poor laddies who steal a few pence.

I feel quite sure that no minister in the country mentioned the fact from his pulpit. I expect they were all too busy anathematising the "Hun" to consider what the attitude of Jesus Christ was to men and women taken in sin. I should like to preach to that School Board from the text "Suffer little children to come unto Me."

There are two ways in education: Macdonalds with Authority in the shape of School Boards and magistrates and prisons to support him; and mine with the Christlike experiment of Homer Lane to encourage me.

I wonder why there are two sides to this question of education? No one but a fool will contend that the birch rod is better than the Little Commonwealth. I think that ninety per cent. of the Macdonalds of Scotland would believe in the Little Commonwealth. Why then would they argue that their system of teaching is better than mine? Obviously coercion and authority make a child less individual than he might be. Ah! it all turns on our respective attitudes to life. "Boys are innately bad," they say, "whack 'em!" "Boys are innately good," I say, "I'll light my pipe and ask them how their rabbits are getting on."

* * * * *

Macdonald came hurrying up to me to-night.

"I quite forgot to ask you when you came down what you used to do about your desk. The lock's broken; how long has it been like that?"

"Since my first week in school," I said.

"Good gracious! Mean to tell me your desk was open for two years?"

I nodded, and smiled at his consternation.

"I've sent down to the joiner. The situation is intolerable. Why, do you know what I found in it to-day?"

"A packet of sweets," I hazarded . . . "chocolates if you were lucky."

"How did you guess?" he cried in amazement.

"My dear fellow, my desk was a sweety shop some days; they used to hide their packets in every corner of it, then they would come to me and say: 'Please, sir, my pockie is in the wee corner on the right; dinna let onybody touch it.' Who put them in?" I asked.

"Gladys Miller."

"You have all the luck," I said. "Gladys always buys liquorice rolls, you know them . . . little yellow sweets with the sugarelly inside. Man, I love yon sweets . . . and Gladys knew it, the besom!"

"Oh! It's all very well for you to make a joke of it," he said with annoyance, "but I tell you I don't like it, and after to-day I guess it'll be a long time till anybody opens my desk again. I talked to Gladys to some tune I can tell you."

I sighed wearily and filled my pipe.

"Two years!" said Macdonald musingly, "two years! What about all your private books? Anybody might have read your Log Book, or destroyed it even!" and the thought almost made him turn pale.

"And what about it? Nobody will ever read it anyway."

"Eh?" His mouth gaped at this latest heresy.

"What about it?" I continued, "what about the whole damned lot of registers and log books and Form 9 b's? I didn't care a rap who saw the inside of my desk or my log book. As a matter of fact no one saw what was in the log; never a child opened it. Why? Because there was no prohibition. You lock up all the blamed things and put the fear of God on any kid that dares touch your desk . . . result! they look on all your belongings as forbidden fruit, and if they can handle your log book when you are safely out of the way you bet your boots that they'll do it. Can't you see that children are really decent kindly creatures with their own philosophy, that is, their own idea of the importance of things? What is important to them is a toy or a dogfight or a quarrel or a love affair. They don't want to touch stodgy official books. But when you say to them: 'This desk is holy ground' why, every self-respecting kid has but one ambition in life . . . to poke his nose into your desk and hide your registers."

"Well," he said with a grim smile, "what about those tools in the woodwork room? If children are the saints you make them out to be, how did your boys come to spoil good tools?"

"I admit that I made a mistake," I said cheerfully. "I set out on the assumption that a boy can be trusted with tools. I dropped the belief. Wood was scarce and often I couldn't get enough to keep the boys working. Result!. . . they took to hammering nails into benches and walls. I see now that much of a boy is destructiveness. I might have known it, for as a boy I tore the inside out of everything to see how it worked. If I had a small class I could have kept them interested in making an article. Yet I remember seeing Tom Watson, the best worker in the school, make a good rabbit-trough; then when he had finished he deliberately chipped a chunk off a plane with a hammer."

"What did you do?"

"I simply chucked him out of woodwork; told him he wasn't beyond the infant-room stage, and gave him lessons with a class two grades below his own."

"Did you chuck him out forcibly?"

"I suppose I did."

"Ah!" Macdonald looked triumphant. "In other words you forgot your principles and punished?"

"Human nature is weak," I said sadly. "If I saw a boy sticking a pen-knife into the tyre of my bicycle I should kick him . . . kick him hard and then kick him again. There is such a thing as elemental rage in every man—even Christ used a whip in the temple. There are times when you cannot reason: you act impulsively. Principle can't touch this, but it comes in when rage is gone. If I am a magistrate and a boy comes before me charged with destroying a bicycle I personally have no rage against the boy, and if I punish him I'm merely serving out juridical vengeance. If I order him to be birched the jailor has no grudge against the boy. The main point is that the owner of the cycle acts before reasoning, while the magistrate acts after reasoning. And his reason cannot prompt him to behave any better than the injured owner did. The owner is primitive man for the time being: the magistrate stands for reasoning civilisation. In other words reasoning civilisation is no better than the barbarian. That's why I object to juridical punishment."

"Ha! Ha!" he laughed with a sneer, "when it touches yourself you let all your principles slide, just as the most extreme Socialist turns Tory if he happens to get money!"

"Macdonald," I said slowly, "I'm sorry you said that, for it means that you'll reject everything I bring forward. You'll grasp the idea that my views are useless because I tell you I can smite when I am angry, and you'll consequently reject everything I say. You're like the man who cries to a Socialist orator: 'Why don't you sell your watch and divide the proceeds among this crowd?' or like the man who tells a member of the no-hat brigade that he should go naked to be consistent. If I were to adopt your tactics I might ask why you don't get the School Boards to provide muzzles for the children on the plea that so much of your energy is taken up in keeping them silent. If you make them salute you I see no logical reason why you shouldn't carry respect to its extreme and force them to kneel down and kiss your boots. If you insist on perfect truthfulness why do you try to hide the truth about the sex of pigeons? You pretend to be a believer in perfect obedience to authority, and yet I saw you ride a bicycle without a light the other night. I am quite willing to prove that every man is inconsistent. Bernard Shaw would no doubt find some difficulty in explaining how his humanitarian vegetarianism blends with his wearing of leather boots; for I don't suppose that he has boots made from the hides of animals that died of old age. I gave up shooting and fishing because I saw that both were cruel, yet I will kill a wasp or a rat on occasion. If a tiger got loose down in the village I should at once borrow Frank Thomson's gun, but I should refuse to go tiger-hunting in Bengal. My dear chap, I am as full of inconsistencies as an egg's full of meat. So are you; so is every man. The best of us are but poor weaklings, for we are each carrying the instincts of millions of our tree- and cave-dwelling ancestors on our backs. My point, however, is that in spite of our weaknesses and animalisms we are predominantly good. I am a caveman once in five years; I am a reasoning humanitarian the rest of the time. You fasten on my elemental side and refuse to think that there can be any good in my humanitarian side.

"You see, I quite earnestly believe that your respect for law and authority is genuine, almost religious, and the fact that I saw you break the law by riding without a light doesn't make me doubt your respect for law."

"I had had a puncture," he explained.

"Exactly! Extenuating circumstances. That's what I might plead when I kick the boy who deliberately punctures my machine . . . but you would laugh. Why, I think I should start in to lecture *you* on your inconsistencies!"

I find that the worst man to answer is the fundamental antagonist. I used to be stumped by the anti-socialist cry: Socialism will destroy enterprise!. . . until I discovered that the best answer to this was: If enterprise has made modern capitalism and industrialism, by all means let it be destroyed. Macdonald will crow over what he considers my failure to be consistent, but it will never once strike him that my frank self-analysis is a thing that he will never practise himself.

Confound Macdonald! He has led me into defending myself; he never defends himself when I attack him; he is far too cocksure to have any doubts about himself.

CHAPTER V.

I am losing Jim Jackson. The battle for his soul is unequal. Macdonald has him all the day, while I only see him at intervals. He came up to the farm to-night, and he was morose in manner. His face is gradually assuming a sneering expression, and his repartee is less spontaneous and more biting. I managed to bring back his better self to-night, but I fear that a day will soon come when he will sink his better self for ever. His father and mother are people after Macdonald's own heart. They are typical village folk, stupid and aggressive. Oh, I loathe the village; it reminds me of George Douglas's Barbie in *The House with the Green Shutters*; it is full of envy and malice and smallness. There are too many "friends" in the village. Mrs. Bell is Mrs. Webster's sister, and they have lived next door to each other for twenty-five years, during which time they have not exchanged a single word. They quarrelled over the division of their mother's goods. When the father dies they will meet and weep together over his coffin; they will be inseparable for a few days . . . then they will have a row over the old grandfather clock, and they won't speak to each other again.

Peter Jackson is a loud-mouthed fool, and his wife is a warrior. She has the jaw of a prize-fighter. Jim was dissecting the front wheel of his old bicycle the other night at the door, and I stopped to give him a hand with the balls. His mother came to the door.

"Jim!" she rasped, "come away to yer bed!"

"Wait till Aw get thae balls in, mother," he pleaded.

"Come away to yer bed this meenute!" she bawled, "or Aw'll gie ye the biggest thrashin' ye ever got in yer life!" And the poor boy had to leave his cycle and obey.

"What about this?" I said to the mother, and I pointed to the cycle.

"He'd no business takin' it to bits," she shouted and she slammed the door.

Poor lad! Between Macdonald and a mother like that he will live hardly. Each will break his will; each will insist on perfect obedience to arbitrary orders. I am honestly amazed at the small success I had with Jim. He was leaving my free school every night to go home to an atmosphere of anger and brutal stupidity. Now he is leaving his poor home every morning to go to the prison of Macdonald. No wonder the lad is lapsing. In a few years he will be a typical villager; he will stand at the brig of an evening and make caustic comments on the passers-by; he will sneer at everything and everybody. Macdonald is thinking about the answering Jim will do when the inspector comes; I was thinking of the Jim that would one day stand at the brig among his acquaintances. I didn't care a brass farthing what he learned or how much he attended; all I tried to do was to help him to be a fine man, a kindly man, a free man.

I recollect a young teacher who visited my school one morning.

"I should like to see you give a lesson," he said.

"With pleasure," I replied.

"What sort of lesson will it be?" he asked, "geography or history?"

"I don't know," I said, and I turned to my bairns.

"Why do rabbits have white tails?" I asked, and from that we wandered on through protective coloration and heredity to wolves and their fear of fire. We finished up with poetry, but I don't recollect how we got to it. When I had finished he pondered for a little.

"It's all wrong," he said. "That boy in the corner was half asleep; four of these girls weren't really attending to you, and two girls left the room."

"My fault," I said. "I took them to subjects they weren't interested in."

"No," he said decidedly, "it was only your fault in not forcing them to sit up and attend."

"But why should I?" I asked wearily. "Schooling is the beginning of the education we call life, and I want to make it as true to life as possible. In after life no one compels my attention or yours. We can sleep in church and we can sleep at a political meeting. We learn lots of things but we are interested in them. Tell me, what boy in this room answered best?"

He pointed to a boy of twelve.

"I agree," I said, and I called the boy to my desk.

"Hugh," I said, "kindly tell this gentleman how long you have been at school."

"A week, sir," he replied.

"What school did you come from?" asked the visitor.

"I never was at any school in my life," he said, "my father lives in a caravan and I never was long enough in a place to go to school."

I explained that Hugh had come voluntarily to me saying: "My father can't read or write, and I can't either, but I want to be able to read about the war and things like that."

"I don't know what to make of it," said my visitor.

"It is a great lesson on education," I said. "He feels that he wants to read . . . and he comes to school seeking knowledge. And that's what I want to supersede compulsion. If I had my way no boy would learn to read a word until he desired to read; no boy would do anything unless he wanted to do it."

Then he brought forward the old argument that freedom like that was handicapping them for after life; they would not face difficulties.

"Hugh was up against a greater difficulty than most boys ever come up against," I said, "and he faced it bravely and confidently. When you are free from authority you have a will of your own; you know exactly what you want and you set your teeth and get it. You are on your own, you have acquired responsibility. Given a dictating teacher or parent a boy will do the minimum on his own responsibility. Good lord! if I make all these youngsters sit up and attend strenuously to my speaking I am not training them to face difficulties; I am simply bullying them, making them a subject race."

"You are training character."

"I would be training children to obey, and the first thing a child should learn is to be a rebel. If a man isn't a rebel by the time he is twenty-five, God help him! Character simply means a man's nature, and I refuse to change a man's nature by force; I leave the experiment to the judges and prison warders."

I want to ask every dominie who believes in coercion what he thinks of the results of many years' coercion. Obviously present-day civilisation with its criminal division of humanity into parasites and slaves is all wrong.

"But," a dominie might cry, "can you definitely blame elementary education for that?"

I answer: "Yes, yes, yes!"

The manhood of Britain to-day has passed through the schools; they have been lulled to sleep; they have never learned to face the awful truth about civilisation. And I blame the coercion of the teachers. Train a boy to obey his teacher and he will naturally obey every dirty politician who has the faculty of rhetoric; he will naturally believe the lies of every dirty newspaper proprietor that is playing his own dirty game.

* * * * *

I have been spending the week-end with a man I used to dig with in London. He is a great raconteur and we sat late swopping yarns.

"Did you ever hear a good yarn without a point?" he asked.

I said that I hadn't.

"Well, I'll tell you one," he said, and he trotted out the following.

In a small seaside town on the east coast an ancient mariner sits on the beach and yarns to visitors. When the Balkan War was going on my friend asked him if he had ever been to Turkey. My friend assured me that the man had never been farther than Newcastle in his life.

"Man," said the mariner reflectively, "Aw mind when an order cam from the Sultan o' Turkey to the sweetie works here for peppermints. The manager cam doon to me and he says to me, says he: 'Man, Jock, Aw wonder if ye would care to tak oot a cargo o' peppermints to the Sultan o' Turkey?'"

"Aweel, the 'Daisy' was lyin' in the harbour at the time, so Aw says that Aw wud tak them oot.

"Weel, we got them aboard, and awa we sailed, and a damned rough passage we had too; man, the Bay o' Biscay was as bad as Aw've ever seen it.

"Weel, we got to Constantinople, and here was the Sultan stannin' on the pier wi' his hands in his breek pooches. He cam aboard and said he wud like to hae a look o' the peppermints. He had a look o' them, and syne he comes up to me and he says: 'Look here, captain, Aw've been haein' a look o' yer crew, and . . . weel, to tell the truth, Aw dinna like the look o' them; there's not wan that Aw wud like to trust up at the harem. So, captain, Aw was just thinkin' that Aw wud like ye to carry up thae peppermints yersel . . . ye're a married man, are ye no?'

"Aw telt him that Aw was, and Aw started to carry up thae peppermints, and a damned hard job it was, man. They werena the ordinary pepperies, ye ken; they were great muckle things like curlin' stanes. Weelaweel, Aw got them a' carried up, and Aw was standin' wipin' the sweat frae my face when the Sultan comes anower to me.

"'Aye, captain,' says he, 'that'll be dry wark?'

"'Yes, sir,' says I, 'gey dry.'

"'Are ye a 'totaller?' says he.

"'No,' says I, and he taks me by the arm and says: 'C'wa and hae a nip!'

"Weel, we gaed into a pub, and he ordered twa nips . . . aye, and damned guid whiskey it was too. We had another twa nips, and Aw'm standin' wi' the Sultan at the door, just aboot to shak hands wi' him, ye ken, and he says to me, says he: 'Captain, wud ye like to see the harem?' and Aw said Aw wud verra much. So he taks haud o' my arm and we goes up the brae. We cam to a great muckle hoose, and he taks a gold key oot o' his pooch, and opens the door.

"Man, Aw never saw the likes o' yon! The floor was a' gold, and the window-blinds was gold. And the wemen! (The mariner conveyed his admiration by a long whistle.)

"Weel, Aw was standin' just inside the door wi' my bonnet in my hand, when a bonny bit lassie comes up to me and threw hersell at my feet and took haud o' my knees and sang: 'Far awa to bonny Scotland!'

"Man, the tears cam into my een as she was singin'.

"Syne the Sultan turns to me.

"'Aye, man,' he says, says he, 'speakin' aboot Scotland: Scotland's the finest country on earth; but there's wan thing Aw canna stand aboot Scotland, and that's yer dawmed green kail. There's no a continental stammick will haud it doon.'"

My friend informed me that he never met an Englishman who appreciated that yarn.

* * * * *

I begin to wonder whether I am falling in love. Ever since Margaret blushed when she passed me on the brae I have been extremely conscious of her existence. I find that I am beginning to look for her, and I go to the dairy on the flimsiest of pretences. I was there three times this afternoon.

"What do you want this time?" she asked with a laugh at my third appearance.

"I hardly know," I said slowly, "but I think I wanted to see your bare arms again."

She hastily drew down her sleeves and reddened; then to cover her confusion she made a show of putting me out forcibly. How I managed to refrain from kissing her tempting lips I don't know. I nearly fell . . . but it suddenly came to me that a kiss might mean so very much to her and so little to me and . . . I resisted the temptation.

She is fast losing her shyness, and she talks to me with growing frankness. She has begun to read much lately, and she devours penny novelettes with avidity. She has a romantic mind, and my realism sometimes shocks her. I happened to meet her in town last Saturday, and I took her to the pictures. She was intensely moved by a romantic film story, and when I explained that the stuff was rank sentimentalism and rhetoric she seemed to be offended.

"You criticise everything," she cried angrily, "don't you believe that there is any good in the world?"

"You will never be happy," she added seriously, "you criticise too much."

"Surely," I cried, "you don't imagine that I criticise you!"

"I do," she said bitterly. "You criticise yourself and me and everybody. I am always in terror that I make a slip in grammar before you."

"Margaret!" I cried with real sorrow, "I hate to think that I have given you that impression."

I was silent for a long time.

"Kid," I said, "you are quite right. I do criticise everything and everybody, but a better word is analyse; I analyse myself and then I try to analyse you."

"As a boy," I added, "my chief pastime was buying sixpenny watches and tearing their insides out to see how they worked . . . but I never saw how they worked."

"Yes," she said, "and that's what you would do if you had a wife; you would tear her to bits just to see how she worked . . . and you would never find out how she worked either."

"Perhaps I might," I said with a smile. "When I dissected watches I was inexperienced; nowadays I could take a watch to pieces and find out how it worked. Perhaps I might manage to put my wife together again, Margaret."

"There would be one or two wheels left over," she laughed.

"I should like her better without them," said I.

"Oh!" she cried impatiently, "why can't you be like other men? What's the use of looking into the inside of everything? Look at father; he never bothered about what mother was; he just thought her perfect and look how happy he is!"

"Ah!" I said teasingly, "I understand! You don't want a man to analyse you in case he discovers that you aren't perfect!"

She looked at me frankly.

"I wouldn't like to be thought perfect," she said slowly. "I sometimes think that mother would think far more of father if he saw some faults in her."

"I am quite puzzled," I said; "you grumble because I analyse people and now you grumble because your father doesn't. What do you mean, child?" But she shook her head helplessly.

"Oh, I don't know," she cried, and she sat for a long time in deep thought.

As I sat by her side in the picture-house tea-room I recollected a saying of her's one day last week. I was sitting at the bothy door reading *The New Age*, and at my feet lay *The Nation* and *The New Statesman*. She picked up *The Nation* and glanced at its pages.

"I don't know why you waste your money on papers like that," she said petulantly. "You spend eighteenpence a week on papers, and father only gets *John Bull* and *The People's Journal*."

It suddenly came to me that Margaret was not thinking of the money side of the question at all; what annoyed her was the thought that these papers were a symbol of a world that she did not know. And now I wonder whether woman is not always jealous of a man's work. It is a long time since I read *Antony and Cleopatra*, but I half fancy that Cleopatra was much more jealous of Antony's work than of his wife.

CHAPTER VI.

Dickie Gibson cut me dead to-night, and I think that Jim Jackson will one day look the other way when I pass. It is very sad, and I feel to-night that all my work was in vain. I cannot, however, blame Macdonald this time, for Dickie has left the school. I feel somewhat grieved at not being able to lay the fault at Macdonald's door. I should blame myself if I honestly could, but I cannot, for Dickie was a lad who loved the school.

I recollect the morning when we arrived to find a huge stone cast in the middle of the pond.

"It's been some of the big lads," said Dickie.

"But why?" I asked. "Why should they do a dirty trick like that? Would you do a thing like that, Dickie, after you had left the school?"

He thought for a minute.

"Aye," he said slowly, "if Aw was with bigger lads and they did it Aw wud do it too."

I suppose that if I had been a really great man I might have conquered the spirit of the village. I was only a poor pioneer striving to make these bairns happier and better. Dickie's cutting me proves that I was not good enough to lead him away from the atmosphere of the village. I used to forget about the homes; I used to forget that many a child had to listen to harsh criticisms of my methods. I marvel now that they were so nice at school. I wonder whether we could not form a Board to enquire into the upbringing of children. We might call it the Board of Parental Control. It would bring parents before it and examine them. Parents convicted of stupidity would be ordered to hand over their children to a Playyard School, and each child would be so taught that it could take in hand the education of its parents when it was seventeen.

My idea was to produce a generation that would be better than the present one, and I thought that I could successfully fight the environment of home. I failed. . . . Dickie has cut me. The fight was unequal; the village won. After all I had Dickie for two short years, and the village has had him for fourteen. Poor boy, he has much good in him, much innate kindliness. But the village is stupid and spiteful. I am absolutely sure that Dickie cut me because he wanted to follow the public opinion of the village.

Am I magnifying a merely personal matter? Am I merely piqued because I was cut? No one likes to be cut; it isn't a compliment at any time. No, I am not piqued: I am intensely angry, not at poor Dickie, but at the dirty environment that makes him a cad. Lucky is the dominie who teaches bairns from good homes. Last summer when I spent half a day in the King Alfred School in Hampstead I envied John Russell his pupils. They were all children of parents who were intellectual enough to seek a free education for their children in a land where the schools are barracks. "If I only had children like these!" I said to him, but a moment later I thought of my little school up north and I said: "No! Mine need freedom more than these."

The King Alfred School is a delightful place. There is co-education . . . a marvellous thing to an Englishman, but not noticeable by a Scot who has never known any other kind. There is no reward and no punishment, no marks, no competition. A child looks on each task as a work of art, and his one desire is to please himself rather than please his teacher. The tone of the school is excellent; the pupils are frankly critical and delightfully self-possessed. And since parents choose this school voluntarily I presume that the education we call home-life is ideal. How easy it must be for John Russell! If my Dickie had been going home each night to a father and mother who were as eager for truth and freedom as I was, I don't think that Dickie would have cut me to-night.

* * * * *

Dickie came up for his milk to-night, and I hailed him as he went down the brae.

"Here, Dickie!" I called, "why have you given up looking at me?"

He grew very red, and he stood kicking a stone with his heel.

"I don't want you to touch your cap, Dickie, but you might at least say Hullo to me in the passing. Some of the big lads who left school before I came look at me impudently, and I know that their look means: 'Bah! I've left the school and I don't care a button for you or any other dominie!' But, Dickie, you know me well; you never were afraid of me, and I know that you don't think me your enemy. Why in all the earth should you pretend that you do?"

I held out my hand.

"Dickie," I said, "are you and I to be friends or not?"

He hesitated for a moment, then he took my hand.

"Friends," he said weakly, and his eyes filled with tears. Then I knew that I had not been mistaken in thinking that there was much good in the boy.

Having made it up with Dickie I set off with a light heart to attend a meeting of the Gifts for Local Soldiers Committee. The chairman was absent and I was invited to take the chair. Bill Watson brought forward a motion that the Committee should get up a concert to provide funds.

"Mr. Watson's proposal is that we arrange a concert," I said. "Is there any seconder?"

"Aweel," said Andrew Findlay, "Aw think that a concert wud be a verra guid thing. The nichts is beginnin' to draw in, and it wud be best to hae it as soon as possible. The tatties will be on in twa three days."

"The proposal is seconded. Any amendment, gentlemen?"

"Man," said Peter MacMannish the cobbler, "man, Aw was just lookin' at Lappiedub's tatties the nicht. Man, yon's a dawmed guid crap."

"Them that's in the wast field is better," said Andrew.

"But the best crap o' wheat Aw seen the year," said Dauvid Peters, "was Torrydyke's."

"Any amendment, gentlemen?"

"Torrydyke ay has graund wheat," said Peter. "D'ye mind yon year—ninety-sax . . . or was it ninety-seeven?—man, they tell me that he made a pile o' siller that year."

"Ninety-sax," growled William Mackenzie the farmer of Brigend, "it was ninety-sax, for Aw mind that my broon coo dee'd that summer."

"Aw mind o' her," nodded Andrew, "grass disease, wasn't it?"

"Aye," said Mackenzie. "Aw sent to Lochars for the vet but he was awa frae hame. Syne Aw sent a telegram to the Wanners vet, and when he cam he says to me, says he—"

"Any amendment, gentlemen?" I said.

"Goad, lads," said Andrew sitting up in his chair, "we'll hae to get on wi' the business."

"No amendment," I said. "Are we all agreed about this concert?" and they grunted their assent.

"And now we'll settle the date," I said briskly.

Peter MacMannish looked over at Mackenzie.

"When are ye thinkin' o' killin' that black swine o' yours, John?" he asked.

Mackenzie growled and shook his head.

"She's no fattenin' up as Aw cud wish to see her, Peter," he replied. There followed an animated discussion of the merits and demerits of various feeding-stuffs. After a two hours' sitting the Committee unanimously appointed me secretary and organiser of the concert. I was given authority to fix a date and arrange a programme.

Attendance at many democratic meetings of this kind has led me to a complete understanding of Parliament.

* * * * *

It is Sunday to-day. I sat reading in the afternoon and a knock came at my bothy door.

"Come in!" I shouted, and Annie walked in.

"Me and Janet and Ellen are going for a walk over the hill, and we thocht you might like to come too."

"Certainly!" I cried, and I threw Shaw's latest volume of plays into the bed.

"Margaret's wi' us too," said Annie as if it were an afterthought.

There was a fight for my arms.

"Annie was first," I said, "and we'll toss up for the other arm."

"Let Margaret get it," said Janet mischievously, and Margaret's nose went almost imperceptibly higher in the air.

"Excellent!" I said, and I took her arm and placed it through mine. Janet and Ellen walked behind, and they sniggered a good deal.

"Just fancy the mester noo!" said Janet, "linkit wi' Maggie! He'll hae to marry her noo, Ellen!" And poor Margaret became very red and began to talk at a great rate.

"G'wa, Jan," I heard Ellen say, "he's far ower auld. Maggie's only twenty next month, and he's—he could be her faither."

"He's no very auld, Ellen; he hasna a mootache yet!"

"Aw wudna like a man wi' a mootache, Jan; Liz Macqueen says that she gave up Jock Wilson cos his mootache was ower kittly."

"Weel, she was tellin' a big lee," said Janet firmly. "If she loved him she wud ha' telt him to shave it off."

We lay down in the wood at the top of the hill. Annie was in a reminiscent mood.

"D'ye mind the letters we used to write to one another?" she asked.

I pretended that I had forgotten them.

"Do ye no mind? One day when I wasna attendin' to the lesson ye wrote 'Annie Miller is sacked' on a bit paper and gave it to me?"

"Ah, yes, I remember, Annie, now that you come to mention it. But I can't remember your reply."

"Aw took another bit o' paper, and Aw wrote: 'Mr. Neill is sacked for not making me attend.'"

"Yes, you besom, I remember now. I'll sack you!" and I rolled her over in the grass.

"There was another letter, Annie," I said, "do you remember it?" and she said "No!" so quickly that I knew she did remember it.

I turned to Margaret.

"Annie came to school one day with her hair most beautifully done in ringlets," I explained, "and of course I fell in love with her at once. I wrote her a letter. . . . 'My Dear Annie, do you think yourself bonny to-day?' and the wee besom replied: 'No, I don't!' Then I wrote her again. . . . 'Do you ever tell lies?' and to this she answered: 'No, never!' Then I calmly handed her the *Life of George Washington*."

"But Aw never read it!" she cried with a gay laugh.

"I know . . . and that's why you have never reformed, my dear kid," I said.

"Ellen," said Janet, "d'ye mind that day when you and me got up and walked oot o' the room?"

"What day was that?" I asked; "you two went out of the room so often that I gave up trying to see you."

"It was the day when a man cam to the schule and stood in the room when ye was teachin' us. There was a new boy, the caravan boy that had never been to schule in his life, and ye said that he was better than any o' us."

"So Jan and me took the tig," said Ellen, "and we went oot and sat on the dike."

Janet hee-heed.

"D'ye mind what we said, Ellen? We said we werena to go back to the schule; we were to go up to Rinsley schule to Mester Lawson."

"Aye," said Ellen, "and we said we wudna gie ye another sweetie . . . no, never!"

"And I suppose you gave me sweeties next day?" I suggested.

"We gave ye a whole ha'penny worth o' chocolate caramels," said Janet. Her head rested on my knee and she smiled up in my face. "Ye were far ower easy wi' us," she said seriously, "we never did half the lessons ye gave us to do."

"I know, Jan, but I didn't particularly want you to do lessons; all I wanted was that you should be Janet Brown and no one else. I wanted you to be a good kind lassie . . . and of course, as you know, I failed." And she pulled my nose at this.

"I didn't like the school when I was there," said Margaret; "I never was so glad in my life as when I was fourteen."

"Poor Margaret," I said, "your schooling should be the pleasantest memory of your life. What you learned from books doesn't matter at all; what matters is what you were. And it seems that memory will bring to you a picture of an unhappy Margaret longing to leave school. What a tragedy!"

"Is being happy the best thing in life?" asked Margaret.

"Not the best," I answered; "the best thing in life is making other people happy . . . and that's what the books mean by 'service.'"

* * * * *

Margaret came over to my bothy to-night to ask if I would help Nancy with her home lessons.

"She's crying like anything," said Margaret.

I went over to the farmhouse. Nancy sat at the kitchen table with her books spread out before her. She was wiping her eyes and looked like beginning to weep again.

"It's her pottery," explained Frank, "she canna get it up at all."

Macdonald had ordered the class to learn the first six verses of Gray's *Elegy*, and threatened dire penalties if each scholar wasn't word perfect.

"I'm afraid I can't help you much, Nancy," I said. "You'll just have to set your teeth and get it up. Don't repeat it line by line; read the six verses over, then read them again, then again. Read them twenty times, then shut the book and imagine the page is before you, and see how much of the stuff you can say." I used to find this method very effectual when I got up long recitations in my younger days.

Macdonald gives his higher classes long poems. They have learned up pages of *Marmion* and pages of *The Lady of the Lake*; and now he is giving them the long and difficult *Elegy*. I must ask him some day what his idea is. I made learning poetry optional when I was in the school. I eschewed all long poems, and I never asked a child to stand up and "say" a piece. My view was that school poetry should be school folk-song; I used to write short pieces on the board and the classes recited them in unison. I gave no hint of expression, for expression should always be a natural thing. I have been timid of expression ever since the day I heard, or rather saw, a youth recite *The Dream of Eugene Aram*. When he came to the climax . . . "And lo! the faithless stream was dry!" I suddenly discovered that I was dry too, and I did not wait until Eugene was led away with "gyves upon his wrists." I once saw Sir Henry Irving in *The Bells*. I was a schoolboy at the time and I straightway spent all my pocket money on books dealing with elocution; I also would tear my hair before the footlights! Looking back now I wonder why Irving bothered with stuff of that sort; why his sense of humour allowed him to grope about the stage for the axe to kill the Polish Jew I don't understand. All that melodramatic romantic business is simply theatrical gush. It appeals to the classes that devour the *Police News*.

Expression when taught is gush. When I gave my bairns a bit of *The Ancient Mariner* the whole crowd brightened up and shouted when they came to the verse:—

> I bit my arm, I sucked the blood
> And cried: "A sail! A sail!"

They understood that part, but they put no special expression into the stanza:—

> All in a hot and copper sky,
> The bloody sun at noon
> Right up above the mast did stand,
> No bigger than the moon.

The boys used to emphasise the adjective in the second line, but that was perhaps natural in a community where strong language is the prerogative of grown-ups. I suppose that a teacher of expression would have pointed out that the right arm must be raised gracefully at the third line, and the voice lowered awfully to show the marvellous significance of the fact that the crudoric sun was no bigger than the moon.

All I tried to give my bairns was an appreciation of rhythm. They loved the trochaic rhythm of a poem, *Marsh Marigolds*, by G. F. Bradby, that I discovered in a school anthology:—

> Slaty skies and a whistling wind and a grim grey land,
> April here with a sullen mind and a frozen hand,
> Hardly a bird with the heart to sing, or a bud that dares to pry,
> Only the plovers hovering,
> On the lonely marsh, with a heavy wing
> And a sad slow cry.

And it used to make me joyful to hear them gallop through Stevenson's delightful *My Ship and I*:—

> Oh! it's I that am the captain of a tidy little ship,
> Of a ship that goes a-sailing on the pond,
> And my ship it keeps a-turning all around and all about,
> But when I'm a little older I shall find the secret out
> How to send my vessel sailing on beyond!

I never gave them a poem that needed any explanation. I picture Macdonald painfully explaining the *Elegy*. . . . "Yes, children, the phrase 'incense-breathing morn' means. . . ." I'm gravelled; I haven't the faintest notion of what the phrase means. Gray annoys me; he is far too perfect for me. I fancy that he rewrote each line about a score of times in his mania for the correct word. Gray is Milton with a dictionary.

I once read that Stevenson studied the dictionary often, used to spend a rainy day reading the thing, and his prose does give me the impression that he cared more for how he said a thing than for the thing itself. I think George Douglas a greater writer; indeed I should call him the greatest novelist Scotland has produced. His style is inevitable; his whole attention seems to be riveted on the matter of his story, and his arresting phrases seem to come from him naturally and thoughtlessly. When you read of Gourlay's agony in Barbie market on the day that his son's disgrace is known to everyone, you see the great hulk of a man, you hear his great breaths . . . you are one of the villagers who peep at him fearfully. Every word is inevitable; the picture is perfect. I should be surprised if anyone told me that Douglas altered a single word after he had written it.

When I want to feel humble I take up *The House with the Green Shutters*. I have read it a score of times, and I hope to read it a score of times again.

CHAPTER VII.

Margaret looked up from the novelette she was reading.

"Are the aristocracy really like what they are in this story?" she asked.

"I don't know," I replied; "I'm not acquainted with the aristocracy, but I should say that they aren't like the aristocracy in that yarn. You see, Margaret, I happen to know some of the men who write these novelettes. Murray is a don at them; he'll turn one out between breakfast and dinner. To the best of my knowledge Murray has never dined in any restaurant more expensive than an A.B.C. shop . . . and his characters always dine at the Ritz."

"But have you never met anybody with a title?"

"I once collided with a man at the British Museum door," I said. "He was a Scot. . . . I know that because neither of us apologised; we merely jerked out 'Oh!' I am almost sure that the man was Sir J. M. Barrie. And I shook hands with two dukes and three lords at a university dinner, but they possibly have forgotten the incident."

No. I don't know the aristocracy well.

I met a titled lady last summer. I was staying at a country house near London, and this lady had the neighbouring house. She came over on the Sunday afternoon. My host informed me that she had lost two sons in the war. After she had gone I was asked what I thought of the English aristocracy, and I gave my opinion in these words:—"To the English aristocracy property alone is sacred. That woman has given the lives of her two sons willingly for her country, but if she were asked to give half an acre of her estate to help pay for the war she would go mad with rage and disgust."

When I heard that lady grumble about the wickedness of the munition-workers. . . . "And, my dear, women in shawls are buying pianos and seal-skin jackets!" . . . I realised how hopeless was the cry of *The New Age* for the Conscription of Wealth. The powerful classes will resist Conscription of Wealth as strenuously as they resist the Germans. Yet the Conscription of Men was in very many cases a Conscription of Wealth. One had only to read the Tribunal cases to discover that thousands of men had to deliver up all their wealth when they joined the army. There was Wrangler the actor; his property was his talent to portray character, and from that he drew his income. His property was conscripted along with him. It was fitting that he should give up all when the State required him to give it up. But the State requires all the wealth of the moneyed classes, and because economic power controls political power the State will not conscript the wealth of its real governors.

I see now that our education is founded on the unpleasant fact that property is more sacred than life. Teachers are encouraged to make their pupils patriotic; every boy must be brought up in the belief that it is great and glorious to die for one's country. A real patriotism would lead a boy to realise that it is a great and glorious thing to live for one's country; the true patriot would teach his lads to make their country a great and glorious country to die for. Somehow our schools for the most part ignore this branch of patriotism; it does not seem so important as the flag-waving and standing to attention that passes for patriotism.

Macdonald is decorating the walls of the school with coloured prints of our warships. "To make them realise how much the navy means to them," he explained to me as I looked at them.

"Excellent!" I said. "The navy deserves all the respect we can give it. But, Macdonald, in your position I should give a further lesson on patriotism; I should point out to these bairns that while the glorious navy is defending our shores from a foreign enemy the enemy within is plundering the nation. I should tell them that under the protection of the navy the profiteers are raising the prices of necessaries hand over fist. All the patriotic flag-waving in the world won't help these bairns to understand that the patriotism of the masses is being exploited by the self-seeking of the dirty few."

Patriotism! We have popular weeklies that endeavour to make the people patriotic. They lash themselves into a fury over momentous questions: The Ich Dien on the crest of the Prince of Wales Must Go; The Duke of So-and-So must have his Garter taken from him; Who was the Spy who sent Kitchener to his doom?

The only way to encourage children to be patriotic is to tell them the sober truth about the important things of life. The invention of the word "shirker" managed to effect that the most timid of men should fight for his country; public opinion will always look after the patriotism necessary for war. But my complaint is that public opinion will not look after the patriotism necessary for peace. If we were all true patriots there would be no slums, no exploitation, no profiteering. And the "patriotic" lesson in school should deal with economics instead of jingo ballads of victories won.

* * * * *

I cycled twelve miles to-night, and I raised a comfortable thirst. When I came to the village I dropped into the Glamis Arms and had a bottle of lager. As I came out I ran into Macdonald.

"Lucky fellow!" he laughed, "you have no position to maintain now and you can afford to quench a thirst!"

"Position be blowed!" I said, "I drink when I'm dry, and I always did. When I was dominie here I dropped in here more than once in the hot weather."

"And they sacked you!"

"Not because of that," I said, "but in spite of it. Believe me it was the one thing that made one or two villagers more amiable to me."

The Scot's attitude to the public-house is entertaining. If you have any position to keep up you must not enter a public-house . . . you must get it in by the dozen. When I first went to London and entered a saloon bar in the Strand I was amazed to find women sitting with their husbands; I was also amazed to find no drunks about. In a Scots bar the most apparent phenomenon is wrangling. I never heard an argument in a London bar, and I have been in many: I never saw a drunk man in London, and I was there for two years.

The public-house in Scotland is not respectable: in England it is. Why this should be I can only guess. The Scot may be a bigger hypocrite than the Englishman; what is more probable is that he may be a harder drinker. In Scotland entering a public-house is synonymous with getting drunk. Yet there are what you might call alcoholic gradations. A respectable farmer may enter a bar without comment, but a teacher must not enter it. He is the guide of the young, and he must be an example. Teachers seldom enter village bars . . . and yet Scotland is notorious for drinking. If the teachers determined to become regular bar customers I conclude that Scotland would drink herself off the face of the map.

I have a theory that the Calvinistic attitude to the public-house is the chief cause of Scots drunkenness. When a Scot enters a bar he knows that he won't have the courage to be seen coming out again . . . and he very naturally says to himself: "Ach, to hell! Aw'll hae another just to fortify mysel' for gaein' oot!" The public-house isn't a public-house at all; it is the most private of houses. Peter Soutar the leading elder in the kirk here always carries a bundle of church magazines in his hand when he enters the Glamis Arms; when the date is past magazine time he enters by the back door. Jeemes Walker the leading Free Kirk elder goes in to read the gospel to old Mrs. Melville the invalid mother of the landlord, and the village is uncharitable enough to remark in his hearing that he really goes to interview his brother "Johnny." I think that it was the doctor who originated that joke.

A public-house is no place for a public man in Scotland.

* * * * *

The opening of the coal mines has brought to the neighbourhood a new type of person. He is usually an engineer who has spent a good few years abroad, and he is usually married . . . very much married. His wife is always a grade above the wife of the engineer next door, and the men appear to spend most of their leisure time in mending quarrels that their wives began. Most of the men are amiable fellows with the minimum of ideas and the maximum of knowledge of fishing and card-playing. They have a certain dignity, and they instantly freeze if you casually ask where such-and-such a light railway is to run.

The wives seem to have no interest other than in servants and their manifold wickedness and cussedness. They hold their noses high when they pass through the village, and they bully the local shopkeepers.

When I was a dominie these women patronised me delightfully, but now that I am a cattleman they are quite frank with me. I puzzled over this for some time, and the solution came to me suddenly. They are all English women, and in the English village the dominie is on very much the same social level as the vicar's gardener.

Mrs. Martinlake likes to chat to me now. She is a middle-aged lady who loves to reminisce about duchesses she has known. She once complained to me because the boys did not touch their caps to her, and on my suggesting that they hadn't been introduced she became very indignant. She called to me this morning as she passed the field I was working in.

"Ah! Good morning! I've been looking for you for a long time. I wanted to tell you how much the children have improved; every village boy touches his cap to me now!" and she laughed gaily.

"Good!" I cried. "If this sort of thing goes on they will be touching their caps to their mothers next."

"And why not?" she demanded with a slight touch of aggression.

I shrugged my shoulders.

"As you say—why not? I think that you ought to persuade your little boy to touch his cap to all the mothers in the village. I notice that he doesn't do it. You take my tip and send him down to Macdonald's school; he'll soon pick it up."

She went off without a word, and I realised that I had been distinctly rude to her. Somehow I felt glad that I had been rude to her.

I told Margaret about the incident afterwards.

"I hate manners, Margaret," I said.

"But," she said wonderingly, "you are very mannerly."

"To you I believe I am, Margaret," I laughed. "But that is because you don't look for manners. Mrs. Martinlake is eternally looking for manners, and to her manners mean respect, deference, boot-licking. She doesn't want the boys to doff their caps to her because she is a woman; no, she wants them to recognise the fact that she is Mrs. Martinlake, self-alleged friend of duchesses. She doesn't care a tu-penny damn for the boys and their lives; she is thinking of Mrs. Martinlake all the time. She once talked to me of the respect due to motherhood . . . and you know that she sacked Liz Smith when she discovered that Liz had had an illegitimate child.

"Women of that type get my back up," I went on. "They are stupid, low-minded, arrogant. They are poor imitations of the Parisian ladies who curled their lips contemptuously at the plebeian rabble that led them to the guillotine. The Parisian ladies had a fine pride of race to redeem their arrogance, but these women have nothing but pride of class. Margaret, if a teacher failed to teach a boy anything except the truth that deference is one of the Seven Deadly Virtues, I should say that that teacher was a successful teacher."

* * * * *

The concert was a success to-night. The singing was good, but the speech of the chairman, Peter MacMannish, was great.

"Ladies and Gentlemen,

"We're a' verra weel pleased to see sik a big turn-oot the nicht. Aw need hardly say onything aboot the object o' this concert, but it's to get a puckle bawbees to send oot a clean pair o' socks and maybe a clean sark to oor local sojers oot in France.—(Cheers).

"Weel, ladies and gentlemen, Aw've made mony a speech on this platform in the days when Aw fought for the Conservative Candidate, Mester Fletcher (cheers, and a voice: 'Gie it a drink, cobbler!')"

The light of battle leapt to Peter's eyes.

"Aw ken that wheezin' Radical's voice!" he cried, "and Aw wud just like to tell that voice that there's no room for Radicals in this war. What was the attitude o' that man's party to Protection? When Mester Chamberlain stood up in Glesga Toon Hall what did he say?" I gently touched Peter on the arm and reminded him of the concert and its object.

"Ladies and Gentlemen, we'll no touch on thae topics here, for ye cam here for another object than to listen to me (several voices: 'Hear, hear!') Afore we begin to the programme Aw wud just like to say that we have to thank oor late dominie for gettin' up this concert. Some o' us had no love for him as a dominie, but Aw say let bygones be bygones. We a' ken that he's no a teacher (laughter), but he's a clever fellow for a' that, and we'll maybe see him in Parliament yet. That hoose has muckle need o' new blood. When Aw think o' Lloyd George and that man Churchill; when Aw see the condeetion they've brocht the country till; when Aw think o' the slack wye they've let the Trade Unions rob the country; when Aw see—" I coughed here, and Peter drew up.

"Weel, Ladies and Gentlemen, this is no a poleetical meetin', and Aw've muckle pleasure in callin' upon Miss Jean Black for a sang," he peered at his programme, "a sang enteeled: A Moonlight Sonnita." Miss Jean Black forthwith sat down at the piano.

During the interval Peter digged me in the ribs.

"What d'ye think o' my suggestion, dominie, eh?"

"What suggestion?"

"Aboot standin' for Parliament. It's a payin' game noo-a-days . . . fower hunner a year and yer tea when the hoose is sittin'. Goad, dominie, think o' sittin' takkin' yer tea wi' Airthur Balfoor!" and he sighed wistfully as a child sighs when it dreams of fairyland and wakes to reality.

"Aye," he said after a long pause, "Aw wance shook hands wi' Joe Chamberlain. His lawware says to him: 'This is Mester MacMannish, wan o' yer chief supporters in the county,' and Aw just taks my hand oot o' my breek pooch. 'Verra pleased to meet ye,' says Aw . . . 'and hoo is yer missis and the bairns?' Man, he lauched at that. Goad he lauched!"

Peter forgot the crowded hall; he stared at the ceiling unseeingly, and he lived over again the greatest day of his life. It was fitting that a Scot should have originated the title "Heroes and Hero-Worship."

CHAPTER VIII.

Macdonald came up to-night. I hadn't seen him for weeks.

"I am making out a scheme of work for the Evening School," he said. "What line did you take?"

"My scheme was simple," I replied, "and luckily I had an inspector who appreciated what I was trying to do. I made the history lessons lessons in elementary political economy. Arithmetic and Algebra were the usual thing."

"What about Reading and Grammar?" he asked.

"We read David Copperfield, and I meant to read a play of Shakespeare and Ibsen's *An Enemy of the People,* but I never found time for them. The class became a sort of debating society. I gave out subjects. We discussed Votes for Women, Should Women Smoke? Is Money the Reward of Ability? I told them about the theory of evolution; I began to trace the history of mankind, or rather tried to make out a likely history, but at the end of the session we hadn't arrived at the dawn of written history."

"Did you find any pupil improving?"

"Macdonald, you are a demon for tangible results. The only tangible result of my heresies I can think of is the fact that Margaret Thomson smokes my cigarettes now."

"Have a look at this scheme," he said, and he handed me a lengthy manuscript. The arithmetic was a detailed list of utilitarian sums . . . how to measure ricks of hay and fields, how to calculate the price of papering walls and so on. My own attitude to utilitarian sums is this: if you know the principles of pure mathematics all these things come easily to you, hence teach pure mathematics and let the utilitarian part take care of itself.

His English part dealt minutely with grammar; he was to give much parsing and analysis; compound sentences were to be broken up into their component parts.

In History he was to do the Stuart Period, and Geography was to cover the whole world "special attention being paid to the agricultural produce of the British Colonies."

"It is a 'correct' scheme," I said.

"Give me your candid opinion of it."

"Well, Macdonald, your ways are not my ways, and candidly I wouldn't teach quite a lot of the stuff you mean to teach. Grammar for instance. What's the use of knowing the parts of a sentence? I don't suppose that Shakespeare knew them. If education is meant to make people think, your Evening School would be much better employed reading books. If you read a lot your grammar takes care of itself.

"The Stuart Period is all right if you don't emphasise the importance of battles and plots. I haven't the faintest notion whether Cromwell won the battle of Marston Moor or lost it, but I have a fair idea of what the constitutional battle meant to England. The political war was over before the first shot was fired; the Civil War was a religious war. If I were you I should take the broad principles of the whole thing and skip all the battles and plots and executions.

"As for the British Colonies and their agriculture you can turn emigration officer if you fancy the job. The idea is good enough. My own personal predilection in geography is the problem of race. I used to tell my pupils about the different 'niggers' I met at the university, and of the detestable attitude of the colonials to these men."

Macdonald shook his head.

"No, no," he said, "a black man isn't as good as a white man."

So we went off at a tangent. I told him that personally I had not enough knowledge of black men to lay down the law about them, but I handed him a very suggestive article in this week's *New Age* on the subject. The writer's theory is that in India black men are ostracised merely because they are a subject race, and he points out that in Germany and France the coloured man is treated as an equal. When I was told by a friend that the natives of India despised Keir Hardie because he carried his own bag off the vessel when he arrived in India I realised that the colour question was too complicated for me to settle. I have a sneaking suspicion that the coloured man is maligned; the average Anglo-Indian is so stupid in his attitude to most things that I can scarcely suspect him of being wise in his attitude to the native. I regret very much that I had not the moral courage to chum up with the coloured man at the university: prejudices leave one after one has left the university.

I wish I knew what Modern Geography means. A few years ago the geography lesson was placed in the hands of the science teacher in our higher grade schools, and the educational papers commenced to talk of isotherms. I have never discovered what an isotherm is; I came very near to discovering once; I asked Dickson, a man of science, what they were, but a girl smiled to me before he got well into the subject (we were in a café), and I never discovered what an isotherm was.

The old-fashioned geography wasn't a bad thing in its way. You got to know where places were, and your newspaper became intelligible. It is true that you wasted many an hour memorising stuff that was of no great importance. I recollect learning that Hexham was noted for hats and gloves. I stopped there once when I was motor-cycling. I asked an aged inhabitant what his town was noted for.

"When I coom to think of it," he said as he scratched his head, "the North Eastern Railway passes through it."

But the old geography familiarised you with the look of the map. Where it failed was in the appeal to the imagination. You learned a lot of facts but you never asked why. I should imagine that the new geography may deal with reasons why; it may enquire into racial differences; it may ask why London is situated where it is, why New York grew so big.

For weeks before I left my school my geography lesson consisted of readings from Foster Fraser's *The Real Siberia*. I began to feel at home in Siberia, and what had been a large ugly chunk of pink on the map of Asia became a real place. There is a scarcity of books of this kind. Every school should have a book on every country written in Fraser's manner. I don't say that Fraser sees very deeply into the life of the Russian. I am quite content with his delightful stories of wayside stations and dirty peasants. He paints the place as it is; if I want to know what the philosophy of the Russian is I can take up Tolstoy or Dostoeivsky or Maxim Gorki.

To return to isotherms . . . well, no, I think I'll get to bed instead.

* * * * *

I was down in the village this morning. A motor-car came up, and two ladies and a gentleman alighted.

"Where is the village school?" asked the gentleman, and I pointed to the ugly pile.

"We are Americans," he drawled in unrequired explanation, "and we've come all the way from Leeds to see the great experiment."

"Yes," said one of the ladies—the pretty one—"we are dying to see the paradise of *A Dominie's Log*. Is it so very wonderful?"

"Marvellous!" I cried. "But the Dominie is a funny sort of chap, sensitive and very shy. You mustn't give him a hint that you know anything about his book; simply say that you want to see a Scots school at work."

They thanked me, and set off for the school.

I loafed about until they returned.

"Well?" I said, "what do you think of it?"

"The fellow is an impostor!" said the man indignantly. "I expected to see them all out of doors chewing gum and sweets, and—"

"There wasn't a chin moving in the whole crowd!" cried the young lady.

"The book was a parcel of lies," said the other lady, "and when I next want a dollar's worth of fiction I reckon I'll plump for Hall Caine or Robert Chambers. The man wouldn't speak."

"I mentioned Dewey's *Schools of To-Day*," said the man, "and he stared at me as if I were talking Greek."

I directed them to the village inn for lunch, and I walked up the brae chuckling.

I had had my dinner, and was having a smoke in the bothy when I heard the American's voice: "We want to see the dominie!" Margaret came to the door, and I walked out into the yard. The trio gasped when they saw me; then the man placed his arms akimbo and looked at me.

"Well I'm damned!" he said with vehemence.

"Not so bad as that," I said with a grin, "*had* is a better word." Then they all began to talk at once.

He explained that he was a lawyer from Baltimore: I told him that his concern about the absence of chewing-gum had led me to conjecture that he manufactured that substance. This seemed to tickle him and he made a note of it.

"Be careful!" smiled the pretty lady—his daughter—, "he'll hand over his notes to the newspaper man when he goes back home."

The lawyer knew something about education, and he told me many things about the new education of America; he was one of the directors of a modern school in his own county.

"Come over to the States," he said with eagerness; "we want men of your ideas over there. I reckon that you and the new schools there don't differ at all."

I gave him my impressions of the American schools described by Dewey in his book.

"It seems to me," I said, "that these schools over-emphasise the 'learn by doing' business. Almost every modern reformer in education talks of 'child processes'; the kindergarten idea is carried all the way. Children are encouraged to shape things with their hands."

"Sure," he said, "but that's only a preliminary to shaping things with their heads."

"I'm not so sure that the one naturally leads to the other," I went on. "Learning by doing is a fine thing, but when little Willie asks why rabbits have white tails the learning by doing business breaks down. In America you have workshops where boys mould metal; you have school farms. But I hold that a child can have all that for years and yet be badly educated."

He looked amazed.

"But I thought that was your line," he said with puzzled expression, "Montessori, and all that kind of thing!"

"I don't know what Montessorianism is," I said; "I have forgotten everything I ever read about Froebel and Pestalozzi. All I know is that reformers want the child to follow its own processes—whatever that phrase may mean. I heartily agree with them when they say that the child should choose its own line, and should discover knowledge for itself. But my point is that a boy may act every incident in history, for instance, and never realise what history means. I can't see the educational value of children acting the incident of Alfred and the burnt cakes."

"Ah! but isn't self-expression a great thing?"

"It is," I answered, "but the actor doesn't express himself. Irving expressed himself . . . and the result was that Shakespeare was Irvingised. A school pageant of the accession of Henry IV. may be a fine spectacle, but it is emphasising all the stuff that doesn't matter a damn in history."

"But," he protested, "it is the stuff that matters to children. You forget that a child isn't a little adult."

"This brings us to the vexed question of the coming in of the adult," I said. "You and I agree that the adult should interfere as little as possible; but the adult will come in in spite of us. Leave children to themselves and they express their personalities the livelong day. Every game is an expression of individuality. The adult steps in and says 'We must guide these children,' and he takes their attention from playing houses to playing scenes from history. And I want to know the educational value of it all."

"It is like travel," he said. "When you travel places become real to you, and when you travel back into mediæval times the whole thing becomes real to you."

"I see your point," I said, "and in a manner I agree with you. But why select pageants? You will agree with me when I say that the condition of the people in feudal times is of far greater importance than the display of a Henry."

"Certainly, I do."

"And the things of real importance in history are incapable of being dramatised. You can make a modern school act the Signing of Magna Charta, but the children won't understand the meaning of Magna Charta any the better. You can't dramatise the Enclosure of the Public Lands in Tudor Times; you can't dramatise the John Ball insurrection; all the acting in the world won't help you to understand the Puritan Revolution."

"You are thinking of children as little adults," he said.

"But they *are* little adults! Every game is an imitation of adult processes; the ring games down at the school there nearly all deal with love and matrimony; the girls make houses and take in lodgers. And if you persuade them to act the part of King Alfred you are encouraging them to be little adults. They are children when they cry and run and jump; whenever they reason they reason as adults. They are very often in the company of adults . . . and that's one of the reasons why you cannot trust what are called child processes. Child processes naturally induce a child to make a row . . . and daddy won't put up with a row. The child cannot escape being a little adult. It's all very well for a Rousseau to deal abstractly with child psychology. I am not Rousseau, and I tackle the lesser problem of adult psychology. The problem before me is—or rather was—painfully concrete. I set out to counteract the adult influence of the home. I saw Peter MacMannish shy divots at the Radical candidate because Peter's father was a Tory; I saw Lizzie Peters put out her tongue at the local Christabel Pankhurst because Lizzie's mother had said forcibly that woman's place is the home."

"I see," said the American thoughtfully, "you used your adult personality on the ground that it was the lesser of two evils? But don't you think that that was a mistake? Was the freedom of behaviour and criticism you allowed them not the best antidote to home prejudices?"

"If the children had not been going to homes at night I should have trusted to freedom alone. As it was the poor bairns were between two fires. I gave them freedom . . . and their parents cursed me. One woman sent a verbal message to me to the effect that I was an idiot; one bright little lassie came to me one day with the words of the woman next door, 'It's just waste o' time attendin' that schule.' Do you imagine that all the child processes in the world could save a child from an environment like that?"

When the American departed he held out his hand.

"I came to see a reformer of child education," he said with a smile, "and I discover that you aren't a reformer of child education at all; your job in life is to run a school for parents."

CHAPTER IX.

The school is closed for the Autumn Holiday . . . commonly called the Tattie Holiday here. Macdonald has gone off to Glasgow. The bigger boys and girls are gathering potatoes in the fields here, and I am driving the tattie digger. At dinnertime they come to the bothy and eat their bread; Mrs. Thomson gives them soup and coffee in the kitchen, but they bring their bowls over to my bothy. Much of the fun has gone out of them; the constant bending makes them very tired, and they drop off to sleep very easily. Janet and Ellen lay in my bed all dinnertime yesterday and slept. Occasionally a boy will sing a song that always crops up at tattie time:—

> O! I'm blyde I'm at the tatties,
> I'm blyde I'm at the tatties,
> I'm blyde I'm at the tatties,
> Wi' auchteenpence a day!

Blyde means glad, but there is but little gladness in the band that trudges up the rigs in the morning twilight.

Jim Jackson is sometimes in good form. He has taken on the swaying gait of the young ploughman; he hasn't got the pockets that are situated in the front of the trousers, but he shoves his hands down the inside instead, and he says: "Ma Goad, you lads, hurry up afore the Boss comes roond wi' the digger again!" They call me the Boss now; Macdonald is the Mester. They seldom mention the school at all; if they do it is to recall some incident that happened in my time. But already the memory of our happy days is becoming hazy; life is too interesting for children to recall memories.

To-day Jim sat and gazed absently at my bothy fire.

"Now, bairns," I said, "Jim's got an idea. Cough it up, Jim."

"Aw was thinkin' o' the tattie-digger," he said slowly; "it seems an awfu' roondaboot wye o' liftin' tatties. Could we no invent a digger that wud hoal the tatties and gaither them at the same time?"

"Laziness is the mother of invention," I remarked.

"But . . . cud a machine no be invented?" he asked.

"You could have a sort o' basket," he went on, "that ceppit a' the tatties as they were thrown oot."

"Dinna haver!" interjected Janet, "it wud cep a' the stanes at the same time."

"If spuds were made o' steel," said Jim, "ye cud draw them oot wi' a magnet."

"And if the sky fell you would catch larks," said I.

"If the sea dried up!" said Ellen, and Jim instantly forgot his patent tattie-digger.

"Crivens! What a fine essay that wud mak! Why did ye no gie us that for an essay?"

"Take it on now," I suggested, but he ignored the suggestion.

"The Mester gae me a book to read in the holidays," he said irrelevantly, "and it's called *Self Help*; it's a' aboot laddies that got on weel."

I ceased to listen to their talk. I thought of Samuel Smiles and his Victorian ideals. The book is iniquitous nowadays; it is the Bible of the individualist. Get on! I'm afraid that Smiles' idea of getting on is still popular in Scotland; the country might well adapt the popular song "Get Out and Get Under," changing it to "Get On or Get Under" and making it the national anthem of Scotland.

I once compared *Self Help* with Lorimer's *Letters of a Self-made Merchant to his Son*, and was struck by the similarity of the ideals. Lorimer's book is an Americanised *Self-help*. Smiles is slightly better. With him getting on means more than the amassing of wealth; it means gaining position, which being interpreted means returning to your native village with prosperous rotundity and a gold chain.

Lorimer has no special interest in gold chains and symbols of wealth; he doesn't care a button for position. He preaches efficiency and power; to him the greatest achievement in life appears to be the packing of the maximum of pig into the minimum of tin in the minimum of time. A business friend of mine tells me that it is the greatest book America has produced. Evidently it didn't require the Lusitania incident to prove that America is a long-suffering nation.

Jim was back to the subject of inventions again.

"Aw read in a paper that there's a fortune waitin' for the man that can invent something to haud breeks up instead o' gallis's."

"Ye cud hae buttons on the foot o' yer sark," suggested Janet.

"Aye," said Jim scornfully, "and if a button cam off what wud haud up yer breeks?"

"Public opinion . . . in this righteous village," I murmured; "it's almost strong enough to hold up any pair of breeks, Jim," but no one understood me.

"Ye cud hae sticks up the side," said Ellen, "and yer breeks wud stand up like fisherman's boots."

"And if ye wanted to bend?" demanded Jim.

Ellen shoved out her tongue at him.

"Ye never said onything aboot bendin', and ye dinna need to bend onywye."

"What aboot when ye're gaitherin' tatties?" crowed Jim.

Ellen tossed her head.

"Aw wasna thinkin' o' the sort o' man that gaithers tatties; Aw was thinkin' o' gentlemen's breeks . . . the kind o' breeks ye'll never hae, Jim Jackson."

Jim sighed and gave me a look which I took to mean: "Women are impossible when it comes to arguing." He thought for a time; then he looked up with twinkling eyes.

"Aw've got it!"

"Well?"

"Do away wi' breeks a'-the-gether, and wear kilts."

"And what will ye do wi' yer hands?" put in Fred Findlay; "there's nae pooches in a kilt."

"Goad, Fred," said Jim, "Aw never thocht o' that; we'll just hae to wrastle on wi' oor breeks and oor gallis's."

"Ye cud wear a belt," suggested Janet.

"And gie mysel' pewmonia! No likely!"

"It's no pewmonia that ye get wearin' a belt," said Janet, "it's a pendicitis."

"G'wa, lassie, what do you ken aboot breeks onywye?"

"Aw ken mair than you do, Jim Jackson. For wan thing Aw ken that it's no a subject ye shud speak aboot afore lassies. Come on, Ellen, we'll go ootside; the conversation's no proper."

Jim glanced at me doubtfully.

"It was her that said that breeks cud be buttoned to yer sark!" he exclaimed. He jumped up and hastened to the door.

"Janet Broon," I heard him cry, "dinna you speak aboot sarks to me again; sarks is no a proper subject o' conversation for young laddies."

I think it was Fletcher of Saltoun who said that he didn't care who made a nation's laws if he made its ballads. To-night I feel that I don't care if Macdonald hears the bairns' opinion of Charles I. so long as I hear their opinion of sarks and breeks.

* * * * *

A Trade Union official delivered a lecture on Labour Aspirations in the village hall to-night. I was sadly disappointed. The man tried to make out that the interests of Capital and Labour are similar.

"We are not out to abolish the capitalist," he said; "all we want is a say in the workshop management. We have nothing to do with the way the employer conducts his business; we want to mind our own business. We want to see men paid a living wage; we want to see. . . ." I ceased to be interested in what the man wanted to see. I fancy that he requires to see a devil of a lot before he is capable of guiding the Trade Unions.

Why are these so-called leaders so poor in intellect? Why are they so fearful of alienating the good opinion of the capitalist? If the Trade Union has any goal at all it surely is the abolition of the capitalist. The leaders crawl to the feet of capital and cry: "For the Lord's sake listen to us! We won't ask much; we won't offend you in the least. We merely want to ask very deferentially that you will see that there is no unemployment after the war. We beseech you to let our stewards have a little say . . . a very little say . . . in the management of the shops. Take your Rent and Interest and Profit as usual; as usual we'll be quite content with what is left over."

If a bull had intelligence he would not allow himself to be led to the shambles. If the Trade Unions had intelligence they would not allow their paid leaders to lead them to the altar.

The lecturer had evidently been told that I was the only Socialist in the village, and he called upon me to say a few words. I have no doubt that later he regretted calling upon me.

"The speaker is modest in his demands," I said. "He has told you what Labour is asking for, and now I'll tell you what I think Labour *should* ask for. Labour's chief aim should be to make the Trade Unions blackleg proof. When they have roped in all the workers they will be able to command anything they like. They should then go to the State and say: 'We want to join forces with the State. Capitalism is un-Christlike, and wasteful, and we must destroy it. We propose to take over the whole concern ourselves; we propose to abolish Rent, Interest, and Profit . . . and Wagery. At present we are selling our labour to the highest bidder, and in the process we are selling our souls along with our bodies. Each industry will conduct its own business, not for profit but for social service; no shareholders will live on our labour; we shall give our members pay instead of wages.'

"Gentlemen, I call an organisation of this kind a Guild, but you can call it what you like. It is the only organisation that will abolish wagery, that is, will prohibit labour from being a commodity obeying the Laws of Supply and Demand."

"What about nationalisation of land and mines and railways?" said the official. "These are on our programme, and they will revolutionise industry."

"Hand over the mines and the railways to the State," I said, "and you have State capitalism. You won't abolish wages; you'll buy the mines and railways, and you'll draw your wages from what is left over after the interest due to the late shareholders is paid."

"Ah!" he interrupted, "you want to confiscate?"

"If necessary, certainly. We have conscripted life because the State required men to give their lives; why not conscript wealth in the same way? The State requires the wealth of the rich, not only for the purpose of paying for the war; it requires it to pay for the peace to come."

"Control of industry by producers has always failed," he said. "*The New Statesman* Supplement on the Control of Industry proved this conclusively."

"Of course it has always failed," I said. "Flying always failed, but the aeroplane experimenters did not sit down and wail: 'It's absolutely no good; men have always failed to fly.' If the Railway Trade Union got the offer of the whole railway system to-morrow to run as it pleased it would make a bonny hash of it. Why? Because management is a skilled business. But if the salaried railway officials had the vision to see that their interests lay with the men instead of with the masters, then you would find a difference. The Trade Unions without the salaried officials are useless.

"I read the Supplement you mention. One of the causes of failure given was that the producers had an interest in the plant and they were always unwilling to scrap machinery in order to introduce better machines."

"That's quite true," he nodded.

"Is it? Why does Bruce the linen manufacturer in the neighbouring town here scrap comparatively new machinery when better inventions come out? He has an interest in the plant, hasn't he? Why then does he not stick to the old methods?"

"He knows that he will gain in the end."

"Exactly. And a society of workers running their own business would not have the gumption to see that the new methods would be a gain in the end?"

"The fact remains that they have tried and failed," he said.

"That merely proves that the workers without their managers are hopeless," I said. "What can you expect from a section of the community that has never been educated? You can't make a man slave ten hours a day for a living wage and then expect him to have the organising ability of Martin the cigar merchant, or the vision of Gamage the universal provider. A rich merchant in London said to me when I asked him point blank if he always thought of his profits: 'Profits be blowed! The great thing is the game of business!' I don't see any reason in the world why the manager of say The Enfield Cycle Company should not be as energetic and as capable if he were managing a factory for the Cycle Guild."

"The workers would interfere with him," said the official; "every workman who had a grudge against him would try to get him put off the managership."

"Lord!" I cried, "for a representative of Labour you seem to have a poor opinion of the democracy you speak for! If that is your attitude to your fellow-workmen I quite understand your modest demands for Labour. If the rank and file of the Trade Unions can't rise higher than squabbling about whether a manager should be sacked or not, the Trade Unions had better content themselves with the programme their leaders have arranged for them. They had better concentrate their attention on trifles like a Minimum Wage or an Old Age Pension."

A disturbing thought comes to me to-night. Democracy means rule by the majority . . . and the majority is always wrong. The only comfort I can find lies in the thought that the majority of to-day represents the opinions of the minority of yesterday. Democracy will always be twenty years behind its time.

* * * * *

To-day has been a very wet Sunday. I did not get up till one o'clock. Margaret came over about tea-time and invited me to sample some drop scones she had been making. She was in a skittish mood, and she began to turn my bothy upside down on the allegation that it was time for autumn cleaning. I ordered her to the door, and she sat down on my bed and laughed at me. I said that I would throw a drop scone at her head if it were not for the danger of shying weights about indiscriminately, and she threw my pillow at me. I rose from my chair and went to her.

"Out you come, you besom!" I cried and I seized her by the shoulders. We struggled . . . and I suddenly realised that as we paused for breath her face was very near mine. I threw my arms around her and kissed her straight on the lips. Then slowly we parted and we stood looking at each other. Her face had become very serious.

"You—you shouldn't have done that!" she gasped.

"Why not?" I asked lamely.

She gazed at me wildly for a long moment; then she rushed from the room.

It happened . . . and I don't believe in crying over spilt milk. If I had been a strong man it wouldn't have happened; if Margaret had not been in that skittish mood it wouldn't have happened. Carlyle says somewhere: "Mighty events turn on a straw; the crossing of a brook decides the conquest of the world." Mighty events! Is this a mighty event? I have kissed many a girl. To me, no; but to Margaret I fear that it is. It was most likely her first kiss since she became a woman. I feel very like Alec D'Urberville, the seducer of Tess, to-night . . . only I don't think I'll take religion as he did and try to lead Margaret to salvation as he did Tess. It suddenly strikes me that I am more like Angel Clare. He was an educated man learning farming; I am an educated man tending cattle. He fell in love with the dairymaid Tess; I. . . . But have I fallen in love with anyone? In general I should say that when a man asks himself whether he is in love or not he is not in love. Love over-rules the head; every marriage means a victory of heart over head. Presumably the men who have no heads make the best lovers. Hamlet could not love Ophelia because he had a head; Romeo loved Juliet because he hadn't a head. The whole problem of H. G. Wells' later novels lies in the fact that his men have heads. They are all analytical . . . and the man who analyses himself always appears before the public as a selfish brute. The analytical man cannot make a martyr of himself; he is a weakling; he has his fun . . . and he pays for it, but he makes a woman pay for it also.

I suppose that in ancient times love was a simple thing. You desired a woman, and you hit her father on the head with a stone axe and carried her off to your cave. In the majority of cases it is a simple business yet; you don't knock your prospective father-in-law on the head with a hatchet; you take a filial interest in your prospective mother-in-law's rheumatics instead. When Smith the shopwalker falls in love with Nancy of the hat department his chief concern is to know how he is going to keep house on his salary. He never sits down of an evening saying to himself: "Now, is Nancy my soul-mate? Is her sense of humour something like my own? May we not be absolutely incompatible in temperament?" Smith hasn't the faintest idea what sort of man he is himself, and if you aren't disturbed by doubts about yourself you won't be disturbed with doubts about your future wife. I should guess that Mr. and Mrs. Smith will live happily together . . . if she is a passable cook.

I fear greatly that the introspective man is doomed to connubial misery. Margaret likes to read penny novelettes, and she will probably take a fancy to Charles Garvice some day soon. She knows nothing about music or painting or literature. Unless we are ragging each other we have not a single topic of common interest; we should certainly bore each other during the first-class honeymoon journey south.

Then why in the name of thunder did I kiss her? I suppose that I kissed her because kissing is more elemental than thinking. When she had rushed out I was joyous in the realisation that her lips were sweet, that her neck was gloriously graceful, that her eyes were deep and wonderful. But now her physical charms have gone with her, and doubts crowd in upon me.

I wonder what she is thinking of! I know that she has no doubts about herself, but I fancy that she has her doubts about me. Poor lassie . . . and well she might!

* * * * *

She was milking to-night. I went over and stood beside her. She looked up, and her eyes shone with a new brightness. She could not meet my gaze, and she flushed and looked the other way.

"Margaret," I said softly, "I love you!"

She held up her lips to me . . . and then I walked out of the byre.

And, you know, I intended to say something very different. I intended to say: "Margaret, I was a fool last night. Try to forget all about it."

I kissed her instead. I'm afraid I was a fool last night, and a fool to-night, and a fool all the time. However, I am a happy fool to-night.

CHAPTER X.

Macdonald has returned. He has brought a man Macduff with him, a college friend of his, and now the headmaster of a big school in Perthshire. He has mentioned Macduff to me more than once. Macduff is his ideal schoolmaster, a stern disciplinarian and a great producer of "results." When they came up to see me to-night Macdonald's face glowed with anticipation; it was evident that he had come to my funeral. Macduff was to slay me, bury me, and write my epitaph. I thought of agreeing with Macduff as much as possible, so as to rob Macdonald of his triumph, but I found it impossible to find more than a few points of agreement. I managed, however, to carry the war into the enemy's camp, and Macduff found himself acting on the defensive more than once.

"I read your *Log*," he said agreeably, "and I must congratulate you on it. I laughed at many of the yarns you have in it."

"The worst of being called a humorist," said I, "is that everybody seizes on your light bits, and ignores your serious bits."

"I didn't ignore your serious bits," he said, "I read them carefully . . . and, to be frank, thought them damned nonsense. You don't mind my saying so, do you?"

"Certainly not, my dear fellow! When you've read the evening paper critics' opinion of yourself you can stand anything. I am all for a free criticism; it lets you know where you stand at once."

We both became very amiable after that, and I offered him a fill of Macdonald's baccy. Then I brought out a bottle of whiskey, and we sat round the bothy fire like brothers.

"And now," I said, "tell me all about the damned nonsensical parts."

"Well," he laughed, "it seems a dirty trick to drink a chap's whiskey and slate his ideas at the same time, doesn't it?"

"It might be worse," I said with a smile; "you might slate his whiskey and drink in his ideas at the same time; and I've never met a man who could stand being accused of keeping bad whiskey, although I know dozens of men who will sit with a grin on their faces while you tear their philosophy of life to pieces."

"They grin at your ignorance, eh?"

"Exactly!"

Macdonald held up his glass to the light and eyed it thoughtfully.

"Macduff's theory is that if you spare the rod you spoil the child," he said.

"Yes," said Macduff, "I agree with old Solomon. You know, it's all very well to be a heretic, but you are up against the wisdom of the ages. All the way from Solomon downwards parents have agreed that youngsters must be trained strictly. You can't smash up the wisdom of the ages as you try to do."

"The wisdom of the ages!" I mused. . . . "When I come to think of it the wisdom of the ages taught men that the earth was flat, that the sun went round the earth, that the touch of a king cured King's Evil. Do you mean to say that because a thing has a tradition behind it it must be believed for ever? Because Solomon said a thing is it eternally true? The wisdom of the ages must be made to give place to the wisdom of the age."

"Then you would have each generation ignore all that had been said by men of previous generations?"

"I don't mean that. By all means find out what wise men of old have said, but don't worship them; be ready all the time to reject their wisdom if you feel you can't agree with it. This using the rod business is a tradition because men found it the easiest method for themselves. A child was weak and he was noisy; the easiest thing to do was to whack the little chap. Do you allow conversation in your school?"

"I do not!" he said grimly.

"And why?"

"They can't work if they are talking."

"And that's your sole reason?"

"Yes."

"If an inspector stood at your desk chatting to you about the war, would you have a silent room?"

"Certainly."

"But why?"

"Oh," he said impatiently, "for various reasons. They aren't there to talk; and they've got to be disciplined, to understand that they are not free to do as they like whenever they like."

"Also," I suggested, "the inspector might be annoyed?"

"There's that in it," he confessed with a little confusion.

"The wisdom of the ages agrees with you," I said, "and I think that in this case the wisdom of the ages is wrong. In the first place I want to know what you're trying to produce."

"Educated citizens," he replied.

"And since the Solomon tradition has been in vogue for quite a long time, do you consider that it has produced educated citizens as yet?"

"More or less," he answered.

"I can't see it," I said. "When nine-tenths of the population of these isles live on the border line of starvation you can't surely argue that they are educated citizens. They are bullied citizens . . . and the first step in the bullying of them was the refusal of authority in the shape of the parent and the pedagogue to spare the rod."

"But look here," he interrupted, "come back to the school. Do you think it wrong for a teacher to compel a boy to attend to a lesson?"

"I do. If he has to be compelled the lesson clearly fails to interest him. I would have childhood a garden in which one could wander wherever one pleased; I would abolish fear and punishment."

"And do you mean to tell me," he demanded, "that a boy will offer to learn his history and geography and arithmetic and grammar of his own free will?"

"It depends on the boy. Here, again, we come up against the wisdom of the ages. The wisdom of the ages has decreed that these subjects are the chief things in education. But are they? I should imagine that it is more important for a boy to know something about feminine psychology than about Henry the Eighth. He will one day be called on to choose a wife, but he'll never be called on to choose a king. Again why should geography be of more importance than anatomy? A man never wants to know where Timbuctoo is, but he very often wants to know whether the pain in his tummy is appendicitis or heartburn."

"Go on!" he laughed, "find a substitute for arithmetic now!"

"Arithmetic," I said, "is the trump card of the man who wants a utilitarian education. I can do lots of sums—Simple Interest, Profit and Loss, Ratio and Proportion, Train Sums, Stream Sums. . . . I could almost do a Cube Root. So far as I can remember I have never had occasion to use arithmetic for any purpose other than adding up money or multiplying a few figures by a few figures. Your utilitarianism somehow leads in the wrong direction most of the time. I was brought up under the wisdom of the ages curriculum, and I'll just give you an idea of some of the things I don't know. I don't know the difference between a mushroom and a toadstool; I haven't the faintest idea of how they make glass or soap or paint or wine or whiskey or beer or paper or candles or matches; I know nothing about the process of law; I don't know what steps one takes to get married or divorced or cremated or naturalised; I don't know the starboard side of a ship; I don't know how a vacuum brake works. I could fill a book with a list of the things I don't know . . . a book as big as the Encyclopædia Britannica.

"What I want to know is this: How are we to determine what things are important to know? From a utilitarian point of view it is more important to know how to get married than how to find the latitude and longitude of Naples. As an exercise of thinking it is quite as important to inquire into the working of a Westinghouse brake as to inquire into the working of a Profit and Loss sum."

"Then what curriculum would you have?"

"I wouldn't have any curriculum. I would allow a boy to learn what he wanted to learn. If he prefers kite-making to sentence-making I want him to choose kite-making. If he wants to catch minnows instead of reading about Napoleon, I say let him do it; he is learning what he wants to learn, and that's exactly what we all do when we leave the compulsion of the schoolroom."

"It won't do!" cried Macduff.

"Look at it in this way," I said. "Suppose I am three stone heavier than you. And suppose that I think it would benefit you if you knew all about—let us say Evolution. I come to you, take you by the back of the neck and say: 'Macduff, you get up the Darwinian Theory word perfect by Monday morning. If you don't I'll bash your head for you.' I reckon that you would call in the police . . . and they would naturally call in the local prison doctor to inquire into my sanity. That is exactly what you are doing in your school . . . only, unfortunately, the police and the prison doctor are on your side. Personally I could make out a strong case for your being certified as a dangerous lunatic with homicidal tendencies."

"Ah!" he said, "but the two cases are different. Your arbitrary insistence on my learning all about Darwin has no right on its side; it's merely your opinion that I should know all about Evolution. But when I make a boy learn his history and grammar I am not acting on my own opinion. Personally I confess that I teach lots of things and don't see the use of them."

"You obey the—er—the wisdom of the ages?"

"I suppose I do."

"Education," I said, "should lead a boy to think for himself, but if teachers refuse to think for themselves in case they disagree with the wisdom of the ages I don't see that they are the men to lead children to think for themselves."

Later we discussed motor-cycles, and I learned many tips from Macduff. He is a mine of information on the subject.

When they had gone I thought out the problem of the curriculum. To abolish the curriculum involves abolishing large classes. I would have classes of not more than a dozen pupils. In the free school I picture, classes would not in fact exist; if there were a hundred and twenty scholars there would be ten teachers. They would act as guides to be consulted when necessary. Each teacher would learn with his or her pupils. A teacher is not an encyclopædia of facts; he is an enquirer.

When we tarred the pigeon-house I did not say: "Now, boys, listen to me, and learn how to put on tar." The boys brought chunks of pitch in their pockets (pretty certainly sneaked from the heaps used for tar-spraying the roads). We got an old pail and melted the solid stuff, then we tried to put it on. The trial was a complete failure; the tar would not run. We sat down to consider the matter.

"Tell you what, boys," said Cheery Smith, "we'll thin it wi' some paraffin."

We thinned it with some paraffin and the stuff ran quite easily.

When I told Macdonald of the incident he cried: "Yes, but think of the time you wasted!"

What's wrong with Macdonald and Macduff is that they know too much to be good teachers. They have nothing to learn. They know all the facts about curriculum subjects; they know exactly what is right and what is wrong; they know that their authority is infallible; they know that swearing is bad, that cap-lifting is good; they know that obedience is a great virtue, that disobedience to their authority is an unforgivable sin. They are the Supermen of education; their attitude to the school is exactly the attitude of Charles I. to his Parliament. They believe in the Divine Right of Dominies. The dominie can do no wrong. Macdonald's bairns consider him something beyond a human being; he knows everything; he is above temptation. He has no weaknesses; his pipe goes into his pocket when he meets a child; he wouldn't allow a child to see him kiss his wife for all the gold in the Bank of England.

But there are expectations down at the schoolhouse. And I would almost sell my soul to be in the classroom on the morning when Macdonald enters it with the word paternity writ large on his prim face. I bet my boots that, without saying a single word, he will manage to give the bairns the impression that he had nothing to do with the affair at all.

* * * * *

A friend of mine, a Londoner, came to stay the week-end with me. To-day we rambled over the hills, and a pair of new boots began to make my friend's feet take on a separate existence. We were about three miles from home, and the prospect of walking that distance painfully was rather disheartening to him. Luckily Moss-side milk cart came along, and the boy asked us if we wanted a lift to the village; he was taking the day's milk to the station.

When we left the cart my friend turned to me in amazement.

"Here," he cried, "didn't you give him something?"

"Good Lord, no!" I laughed.

"Oh, you blooming Scotchman!" he said with fervour. "If I had known I'd have given the chap a tip myself."

"I never thought of tipping him," I said, "and if I had I wouldn't have tipped him all the same. You blessed Englishmen can never rise above your stupid feudal idea of rewarding the lower classes. In your south country a countryman is a Lick-spittle; he touches his cap to anything with a collar on. We don't breed that kind of specimen in Scotland. That young lad is a stranger to me, but he and you and I were equals; there was no servility about him; he chatted to us as an equal. He expected nothing, and if you had offered him a shilling you would have patronised him, posed as his superior."

"But, damn it all, the chap earned a bob!"

"He didn't; all he earned was your gratitude. The boy was doing a decent kindly thing for its own sake, and you want to shove a vulgar tip into his hand. If I had come along in a Rolls-Royce car and given you a lift, would you have offered to reward me? What's wrong with you southerners is that you always think in classes; your tipping isn't kindness; you tip to save your self-respect; you are afraid that any man of the lower orders should think you mean. The Scot is not as a rule hampered by class distinctions, and he often refuses to tip because he hates to insult a man. You Londoners put it down to meanness, but I would have felt myself the meanest of low cads if I had tipped that ploughboy. Scotland is comparatively free from the rotten tipping habit. A few gamekeepers get tips from English sporting gentlemen, and a few porters get tips from English travellers."

"You have spoilt that boy for the next unfortunate pedestrian," he said; "the next time he sees a man limping along the road he will say to himself: 'Never again!'" I knew then that he had not been listening to my argument.

If tipping is degrading to the man who tips and the man who holds out his palm, I cannot see that school prize-giving is any better. The kindly School Board members who are anxious to encourage the bairns to work for prizes have essentially the same outlook as my friend from town. I fancy that the modern interpretation of Christianity has something to do with this national desire for reward and punishment. To me the whole attitude is distasteful. Obviously I am what I am; I was born with a certain nature, and I was brought up in a certain environment. The making of my ego was a thing outside my direction altogether. To reward me in an after life for being a religious man is as unfair as to punish me for being a thief. We don't award a gold medal to an actress for being beautiful; we don't offer Shaw a peerage because he is Christlike enough to hate killing animals for sport. Shaw can no more help being humanitarian than Gladys Cooper can help being bonny. Down in the school there Ellen Smith can no more help being the best arithmetician than Dave Ramsay can help being the biggest coward.

Speaking of Dave . . . when Macdonald was worrying over the allocation of prizes the other week, he asked me if Dave was good at anything.

"Well," I said, "he holds the record for spitting farther than any boy in the school; I think he deserves a prize for that. Believe me, Macdonald, every boy in the class would rather hold that record than carry off the prize for arithmetic . . . and I don't blame them either."

The subject of Scots and tipping puts me in mind of what is probably the best "Scot in London" yarn.

A Scot, followed by his five children, entered the Ritz Hotel, and sat down in the lounge.

"Waiter! A bottle o' leemonade and sax tumblers!" he cried.

The waiter was too dumbfounded to do anything but bring the liquor. He stood in open-mouthed amazement as the Scot divided the bottle among the six glasses, but, when the Scot took a bag of buns from his pocket and proceeded to distribute them, the waiter set off blindly to find the manager.

The manager approached. He tapped the Scot on the shoulder, and in a stern voice he said: "Excuse me, but I'm the manager of this establishment."

The Scot looked up at him sharply.

"O, ye're the manager, are ye? Weel, why the hell's the band's no playin'?"

CHAPTER XI.

Macdonald had a sort of cookie shine to-night, and I was invited. The other guests were Mitchell, the assistant-manager of the railway construction department, and Willis, the head of the water department. We played Bridge, and I spent four hours of misery. I hate cards; I can't concentrate at all, and I never have the faintest idea what the man on my left has discarded. Willis and I won.

I always look upon cards as a veiled insult to guests. I want to know what a man is thinking when I meet him; on the few occasions on which I have brought out a pack of cards to entertain guests I have done so on the frank realisation that their conversation wasn't worth listening to.

Later when we sat round the fire to chat I grudged the time lost over the game. Mitchell had been for many years in India, and his stories of life there were of great interest to me. He did not theorise about India; he accepted without thought the attitude of the average Anglo-Indian . . . the nigger is a beast that has to be knocked into shape; the Anglo-Indian mode of government was tip-top, couldn't be beat; asses like Keir Hardie ought never to be allowed to put their foot in India; what's wrong with India is what's wrong with the working classes here—we give 'em too much education, make 'em discontented.

Willis was of a more intelligent type. He had been all over the world, and, although a Conservative to the backbone, he had made some study of modern problems. He had studied Socialism, thought it a fine thing, but. . . . "You've got to change human nature first," he said.

* * * * *

If I were writing a novel I should now head a chapter thus:—Chapter XXIV., in Which Macdonald and I become Brothers in Affliction.

He came up to see me to-night.

"You've put your foot in it this time," he began.

"What is it?" I cried in alarm.

"Old Brown—Violet's father—wants to slay you. His wife heard from Mrs. Wylie that you said to Wylie that he, Brown, had the intellect of a boiled rabbit."

"That's bad," I said in dismay. "The old fool was talking puerile rubbish about the wickedness of the working-classes. Wylie was there, and after Brown had gone I did make the impatient remark that he had the intellect of a boiled rabbit. But, Good Lord! I didn't want the thing to go back to his ears. How I can ever look the man in the face again I don't know."

"You should have thought of that before you spoke," said Macdonald with a smile.

"Oh," I replied, "I don't regret saying it in the least; at the time I felt it was the only thing to say. What I regret is the meanness of Wylie or his wife. Brown is a decent old chap, and I'm rather fond of him. Why the devil are people so dirty in mind, Macdonald? We all say things that we don't want carried to the person we are speaking about. I say things about you that I would hate you to hear, and I guess that you are in a similar position with regard to me. But the unpardonable social crime is to tell one man what another has said about him. It's the lowest down trick I know."

"What'll you do about it?"

"I'll go straight down to Brown and apologise for Wylie's bad taste."

"And your own!"

"Not at all. I'll tell him I've said worse things than that about him, but I'll implore him not to let them make any difference in our friendship."

"I've got a nasty little problem myself," said Macdonald. "You know that confounded committee of villagers that has charge of the Soup Kitchen Fund?"

"I do," I cried fervently.

"Well, I called a meeting for last night . . . and I forgot to post Mrs. Wylie's invitation."

"Call that a nasty problem?" I cried; "my dear chap, you've raised a whirlwind and tempest combined . . . and there won't be any still small voice at the end of 'em either. You've committed the Unforgivable Sin this time."

"She's in an awful wax," he continued; "says that she never was insulted like this before. She came up to-night and gave me beans . . . told me that you were a perfect gentleman!"

"I took care never to omit her when I called the committee," I said modestly.

"She'll never forgive me," said Macdonald dolefully.

"Oh, yes she will . . . if you play your cards well. Your game is to send a notice of the meeting to the local paper. Then commence a new paragraph thus:—The Convener, Mr. Macdonald, intimated that Mrs. Wylie's invitation to the meeting had been unintentionally overlooked, and he expressed his very earnest regret that his mistake had deprived the meeting of the always helpful advice of the injured lady.

"Publicity salves all wounds in the village, Macdonald. Do as I suggest and Mrs. W. will support you for all eternity."

"They are so small-minded," he said.

"They are hyper-sensitive," said I. "Mrs. Wylie is quite sure that you made a mistake. She can forgive you for that, but the thing that she will find it hard to forgive is the fact that you did not pay special attention to her letter, send it by registered post as it were. No one who knows me would accuse me of self-depreciation, but I tell you, Macdonald, every villager down there has more self-appreciation in his little finger than I have in my whole body. Old Jake Baffers never had a bath in his life, and he would be secretly proud of his record if an urchin were to shout at him: 'G'wa and tak a wash!' Yet if the secretary forgot to send him a notice of the Parish Council Meeting Jake would hate the man for all eternity."

"What does it all mean?" asked Macdonald.

"The innate love of publicity lies at the root of all the village hate and narrowness. They spend their little lives looking for trouble, and the trouble they look for specially is a personal slight. The village is always full of this kind of trouble. They like to have a finger in every pie. You don't want them to run your Soup Kitchen; you could do it fifty times better yourself."

"Perhaps they think I'd sneak the cash, eh?"

"No! No, to give them their due, they don't think that. You may rob the Committee of all their cash if you like (think of the fine talk they would have over it!); what you mustn't do is to rob them of their publicity. Some of them will always hate you because you wear a linen collar and don't talk dialect. Also, you are an incomer. I once attended a public meeting in a Fife village. A man stood up to give his opinion about a public matter, and they shouted him down with the cry: 'Sit doon! Ye're an incomer!' The man had been resident in that village for twenty-three years, but he had come from Forfarshire originally."

"And this is democracy!" exclaimed Macdonald.

"This is education," said I. "All the history and geography and grammar in the world won't produce a better generation in this village. What is really wrong is narrow vision due to lack of wide interest. Obviously the village thinks of small things, things that don't count to us. The villager left school at fourteen and he never had any training in thinking."

"Well, and what's the remedy?"

"Remedy be blowed!" I cried. "Come on, I'm going down with you and I'll have it out with old Brown."

* * * * *

Brown was in no mood to be friendly. Indeed he was quite nasty. He told me frankly that our friendship was at an end, and I felt pained about the matter. Suddenly a brilliant inspiration came to me. As I stood at the door I turned to him sharply.

"You've had your say, Mr. Brown," I said sternly, "and now it's my innings. I didn't mean to mention it, but you've forced me to do it."

I paused to note his sudden look of alarm.

"Yes," I went on, "I want to know what the devil you meant by saying that I suffered from swelled head?"

"When did I say that?" he stammered.

I shrugged my shoulders.

"I refuse to give away the man who told me," I said stiffly.

He was now in great excitement. He wiped his brow with his hand.

"Graham is a liar!" he cried passionately, "it was *him* that said it to *me*!"

"But you agreed with him?" I insinuated.

Brown drew himself up stiffly.

"Well, damn you, I did!"

"Quits!" I cried, and I held out my hand.

Later as we sat together over a hot whiskey I tried hard to persuade him that Graham had never said a word to me; I told him again and again that I had made a lucky guess, and at last I managed to persuade him to believe me. Yet somehow I feel that he'll look askance at poor Graham the next time he meets him.

* * * * *

We were threshing to-day. During the dinner interval Margaret and I chanced to meet in the barn. I threw my arms round her and kissed her. A chuckle came from the straw. I looked up to find the eyes of Jim Jackson upon us.

"Aw'll no tell!" he cried, and Margaret fled blushing from the barn.

"Right, Jim! We'll trust you with the secret. Margaret and I are in love with each other."

"When is it to be?" he asked eagerly.

"You are thinking of the wedding feast I presume, my lad, what?"

He did not answer; he seemed to be thinking.

"Bob Scott has a' the luck," he said dolefully; "when he was ten his mither was married, when he was eleven his sister Bets dee'd, and syne when he was twel his father was married. Aw've only had a marriage and a daith. Aw like marriages better gyn daiths; ye get mair to eat, and ye dinna hae to look solemn. A christenin' doesna coont; ye jest get a wee bit o' cake, and the minister prays."

"Jim," I said suddenly, "will you be my best man?"

He gaped.

"Will Aw be yer—?" He was too much surprised to complete the sentence.

"Yes, and carry the ring," I said.

His eyes danced.

"And kiss the bridesmaids," I continued.

His face fell.

"No," he said slowly, "Aw'm ower young to be a best man." He considered for a while. "But Geordie Tamson wud kiss them for a hank o' candy," he said half aloud.

"No," I said, "you can't delegate your powers to another in a case of this sort. But of course if you think Geordie would be the better man to sit on the dickey of the carriage, and lead the bride to the wedding feast, and throw out the sweeties and pennies to the children, and—"

"Aw'll be yer best man!" he roared.

CHAPTER XII.

To-night I made up my mind to speak to Frank Thomson and his wife. I knew that Jim would be miserable as long as he carried so weighty a secret on him; I knew that he was itching to rush through the village shouting: "The Mester's gaein' to be married to Maggie Tamson . . . and Aw'm to be his best man!"

I went over about eight o'clock. The children were in bed, and Margaret sat in the kitchen with her father and mother.

"I want to marry Margaret," I said when I entered.

Frank was reading *The People's Journal*. The paper fluttered slightly, and that was the only sign of surprise that came from him.

"Yea, Mester?" he said slowly. "Man, d'ye tell me that na? Aw see that the Roosians are makin' some progress again." He buried his head in his paper after throwing a look to his wife. The look clearly meant: "This is a matter for you to tak up, Lizzie."

Mrs. Thomson laid down her knitting carefully; then she rubbed her glasses with her apron. She glanced at Margaret, and Margaret rose and left the room quietly. I knew that she left the door half-closed so that she might hear from the stair-foot.

Her mother looked at me over her glasses.

"She's gey young," she said.

"A year older than you were when you married," I said with a smile.

She sat in deep thought for a long time. Then she turned to her husband.

"Frank," she said in a matter-of-fact voice, "ye'll better bring oot the whiskey."

That was all. Neither of them asked a question about my financial position, or my hopes. Mrs. Thomson went to the door and called Margaret's name, and when she entered the kitchen her mother simply said: "Maggie, ye micht bring a few coals like a lassie."

A stranger from a foreign land looking on would have wondered at the unconcern of the whole thing. The family talked about everything but the subject of the moment, but I knew by the way in which they made conversation that they were striving to hide their real feelings.

When I rose to leave I turned to Frank.

"I don't know what plans I have," I said, "but the chances are that I'll go to live in London some day soon."

Frank waved a protesting hand.

"Never mind that ee'noo," he cried. "Maggie!. . . ye'll better see the Mester to the door, lassie!"

"They're awfu' pleased!" whispered Margaret at the door.

"Are they, Margaret?" I said tenderly.

"Yes! But it isn't because you are so clever, you know!"

"Rather because I am so handsome?"

"No. They're pleased because you are an M.A."

Then she laughed at my look of chagrin.

* * * * *

This morning I met Jim.

"Jim," I said, "you are free to speak now."

He made no reply; he sprang over a gate and flew towards the village.

The girls came up in a body at four o'clock.

"Is't true?" cried Janet as she ran up breathlessly.

"What? Is what true?"

"That you and Maggie are to be married?"

"The answer is in the affirmative," I said pompously.

Janet's face fell.

"Eh, if Aw had that Jim Jackson! He telt us that he was to be yer best man!"

"He was aye a big leer!" cried Ellen, then she saw that I was smiling.

"It's true after a'!" she cried.

"Yes," I said, "it's true, bairns," but to my surprise they rushed off and left me. I understood their action when I turned to look; they had seen Margaret emerge from the kitchen door. Poor Margaret! The whole crowd of them insisted on pinching her arms for luck. They seemed to have forgotten my existence; then suddenly they all came running towards me.

"Let me tell 'im, Jan!" I heard Annie cry, but Jan tore herself from restraining arms and was first to come up.

"The Mester's gotten a little baby!" cried Janet.

"Janet's wrang!" cried Annie; "it's no the Mester: it's his wife!"

I tried to look my surprise.

"And did you congratulate him, Jan?" I asked.

Janet tittered.

"He took an awfu' reid face when he cam in this mornin', did'n he, Jean?"

"Aye, and he was grumpy a' day. He was ay frownin' at a' body. We cudna help his wife haein' a bairn!"

"He looked as if he was angry at his wife haein' the bairn," said Barbara.

I recalled my conjecture that he would try to give the bairns the impression that he had nothing whatever to do with the affair, and I laughed uproariously.

I suddenly realised that Gladys was asking me a question.

"Eh? What's that, Gladys?"

"I was speerin' if you and Maggie are to hae a bairn?"

Janet gasped and cried: "Oh, Gladys!" and Jean cried: "Look at Maggie blushin'!"

"Certainly!" I said with a laugh, "a dozen of them, won't we, Margaret?"

"Bairns is just a scunner," said Sarah. "Ye'll hae to stop yer typewriter or ye'll waken them."

"That's awkward, Sarah," I said, "for if I stop my typewriter I'll starve them."

"The Mester'll hae a big hoose," said Jean, "and he'll type his letters in the parlour and Maggie'll rock the cradle in the kitchen, winna ye, Maggie?"

"Perhaps," I suggested, "Jim Jackson will be able to invent a patent that will enable me to rock the cradle as I strike the keys."

"Aye," said Janet with scorn, "and kill the bairn! Aw wudna trust Jim Jackson wi' ony bairn o' mine . . . him and his inventions!"

"Ye'll mak a nice father," said Gladys, and she put her arm round my neck.

"Ye'll spoil yer bairns," said Ellen. She turned to Margaret. "Maggie, dinna let him tak chairge o' them, or he'll mak them catch minnows a' day instead o' learnin' their lessons."

"G'wa, Ellen," cried Sarah, "they're no married yet! And ye dinna get bairns till ye're married a gey lang time."

"Some fowk has them afore they get married," said Barbara thoughtfully, and I chuckled when I saw how the others looked at her. Disapproval was writ large on their faces.

"Ye shudna mention sic things afore Maggie!" said Janet in a stage whisper, and I had to hold my sides. Margaret could not keep her gravity either, and she laughed immoderately.

Later they pleaded with me to tell them when the wedding was to take place. I told them that I did not know, but that it would be soon, and I promised to invite them all.

"But no Mester Macdonald!" said Jean. "Aw wudna feel so free wi' him there."

I told them of the widower whose friends tried to persuade him to take his mother-in-law with him in the front funeral coach. After some persuasion he said resignedly: "Verra weel, then; but it'll spoil my day." Then I sent them home.

* * * * *

The story I told the girls set me thinking of funeral stories. I have heard dozens of them, but the only other one I can remember is the one about the farmer whose wife was to be buried. As the men carried the coffin along the passage they stumbled, and the coffin came into violent contact with the corner. The lid flew off, and the wife sat up and rubbed her eyes. She had been in a trance.

Twenty years later the wife died again. The men were carrying the coffin through the passage when the farmer rushed forward.

"Canny, lads!" he cried, "canny wi' that corner!"

* * * * *

"Look here," said Macdonald to me to-night, "the School Board election is coming off soon; why don't you stand?"

"I thought that I would be the last man on earth you would want on the School Board," I replied.

"Not at all," he said with a smile. "You and I differ about education, but our difference isn't so great as the difference between me and men like Peter Mitchell."

I thought to myself that the difference between his idea and mine was infinitely greater than the difference between his idea and Peter Mitchell's, but I said: "It's very decent of you to suggest it, old chap, but I'm not standing."

"But why not?"

"Possibly for the same reason that H. G. Wells and A. R. Orage and Bernard Shaw and G. K. Chesterton don't stand for Parliament."

"You place yourself in good company!" he laughed.

"I'm not claiming kindred, Macdonald; what I mean to suggest is that I stand to Peter Mitchell and Co. very much in the same relationship as Shaw and Orage stand to Lloyd George and Co. Roughly there are two types of mind, the thinkers and the doers. Orage has better ideas than Lloyd George, but I fancy that Lloyd George is the better man to run a Ministry of Munitions. I've got better ideas than Peter Mitchell (I think you'll grant that), yet Peter is probably the better man to arrange for the gravelling of the playground."

I smoked for a while in silence.

"The best men don't enter public life," I continued. "No man with a real passion for ideas could tolerate the jobbery and gabble of the House of Commons. Public life is for the most part concerned with small things. The Cabinet settles mighty things like war and peace, but if you read Hansard you'll find that ninety-nine per cent. of the members' speeches deal with little things like Old Age Pensions or the working of the Insurance Act. So in the School Board you have to deal with the incidental things. The Scotch Education Department settles the broad lines of education, and the local School Boards simply administer the Education Act of 1908. What could I do on the Board anyway?. . . arrange for the closing of the school at the tattie holidays, discuss your application for a rise in screw, grant a certain amount of money for prizes. I couldn't persuade the Board to convert your school into a Neo-Montessorian Play-Garden; if I did persuade them the Department would very likely step in and protest. Besides I haven't the type of mind. I hate all the formalism of public meetings; I had enough of it at the 'varsity to last me a life time; the debating societies spent most of their time reading minutes and moving 'the previous question.' I'm not a practical man, Macdonald. In art I like pure black and white work, and I think in black and white; I see the broad effect without noting the detail. Detail gives me a headache, and the public man must have something like a passion for detail. Look at the Scotch Education Department; it is full of splendid officials who will spend a week nosing out an error of ten attendances in an unfortunate dominie's registers. That's what should be; the official should have the mind of a ready-reckoner . . . rather, he must have, else he would drown himself after a day in Whitehall."

Macdonald has a passion for detail, and I smiled to note a growing look of aggression on his face.

"Somebody's got to do the detail work," he growled.

"Most of it could very well be left undone," I suggested. "You have to calculate laboriously all the attendances for the year, how many have left school, how many are of such and such an age, and so on. What for? Simply to allow the busy officials of Whitehall to settle what grant should be paid."

"How could they settle it otherwise?" he asked.

"In fifty ways. The obvious way is to find out how much the school requires to run it each year. I would go the length of abolishing the daily register. You don't call the roll in a cinema house or a kirk or a political meeting. Why, man, in the big schools in the cities the headmaster is a junior clerk; his whole time is spent in making up statistical returns for the Department."

"You couldn't get on without the returns," said Macdonald.

"Possibly not at present," I said, "seeing that the system of grants obtains, but if an Education Guild of Teachers controlled the education of Scotland most of the returns could be scrapped. All the returns needed for your school would be a list of expenditure on salaries, books, etc.; main headquarters would control the broad policy and pay the bills."

"And attendance wouldn't count?"

"Not if I had any say in the matter. To have an average attendance of 96 per cent. is about the lowest ideal a dominie can aim at. The teachers and the school boards aim at a high average because of the higher grant; the Department, with an eye on Blue Book statistics, encourages them to aim at a high average because a high average means a country with the minimum of illiteracy."

"Would you abolish compulsory attendance?"

"Certainly—so far as the children are concerned. Make their schools playgrounds instead of prisons, and you'll have no truancy. But I would have compulsion for parents. The State should have the power to say to parents: 'You are only the guardians of these children, and we can't allow you to keep them from education to do your work for you.'"

"You aren't consistent," he said, "here you are advocating Authority!"

"Macdonald," I said wearily, "you must have authority and law of a kind. You must have a law that you take the left side of the road when you are cycling for instance. You must give the community power to overpower a man like that lunatic who assaulted Mary Ramsay the other day, and if the community feels that it must protect children from assaults on their bodies, surely to goodness it must step in and protect little children when parents try to commit assaults on their souls. Compulsion should step in to destroy compulsion."

"Now, what in all the earth do you mean by that?"

"A man compels his son to stay from school; the compulsion of the State overrules the compulsion of the father. So with compulsion of men for military purposes; in theory at least the Military Service Act compels men to fight in order that they may overrule the compulsion that Germany is trying to force on Europe. The Fatherland and the father are interfering with human souls, but if a boy does not want to go to school he is a free agent choosing as he wills, and interfering with the soul of no one."

"What about his children coming after him?"

"A good point," I cried; "in other words you mean that no man liveth unto himself and no man dieth unto himself, eh? Yes, that's quite true, but we don't know what the boy is to turn out. Given a home of comfort and food . . . as every boy would have in a well-ordered community . . . I think that the lad who could resist the attraction of a play-garden school with its charms of social intercourse with other children would be either a lunatic or a genius. Besides we have given up the idea in other departments. I expect that the community is of opinion that the teachings of Christianity are good for a man to hand on to his children, yet I don't think that the community would pass a law that every parent must send his family to a Sunday School. The whole trend of society is to recognise and provide for the conscientious objector, and society should certainly recognise the conscientious objector to school-going."

"A boy doesn't know his own mind."

"Neither do I," I sighed. "I can't make up my mind about anything; rather, I make up my mind to-day and change it to-morrow. And I don't want it to be otherwise; when my opinions become definite and fixed I shall be dead spiritually. The boy doesn't know his own mind! Well, how the deuce can I claim to help him to make it up when I can't make up my own? It's his mind, not mine. I don't mind telling him what I think of a subject, but I wouldn't compel him to do a blamed thing."

"You have a queer idea of education," he said with a dry laugh.

"Macdonald," I said, with real modesty, "I don't know that I have any idea of education. I am simply groping. I don't exactly know what I want, but I have a pretty definite notion of what I don't want . . . and that is finality. I begin to think that what I want education to do is to train men not to make up their minds about anything."

Macdonald rose to go.

"Matrimony does that, old chap," he said with a chuckle, "and you'll soon discover that you won't get the chance of making up your mind ever."

CHAPTER XIII.

I feared that I was losing Jim and Janet and the others, but I have not lost them. They conform to Macdonald's reign of authority when they are in school, but they do it with their tongues in their cheeks. But only the select few have followed my banner. Jim is the only boy, and the only girls are Janet, Jean, Ellen, Annie, and Gladys. Barbara is of divided allegiance. The others are Macdonaldised. I find it a very difficult thing to define Macdonaldisation. Possibly its most distinguishing characteristic is what I might call a dour pertness. The bairns have lost their standard of values; they don't know limits. I pinched Mary's cheek when I met her this morning on her way to school, and she tossed her head in the air and looked at me with a cheeky expression which meant: "What do you think you're doing?" If I rag Eva she answers with brazen impudence. I have given up speaking facetiously to the boys, for they also were impudent. They were not like that when I had them; I could play with them, joke with them, rag them and they took it all with the best good humour; they teased me and played jokes on me, but they did it in the right spirit.

I have seen it again and again. Strict discipline destroys a child's values of good taste and bad taste. Naturally when freedom is denied them they do not know what freedom means. The atrocities committed by the super-disciplined German army are quite understandable to me; like Macdonaldised bairns they did not understand the freedom they suddenly found themselves enjoying, and they converted it into licence. I can tell the character of a village dominie when I stop to ask a group of boys the way to the next village when I am cycling.

Jimmy Young slouches past me now with a stare of hostility, and it isn't six months ago since he came running to me on the road one night for protection from the policeman who was after him for stealing a turnip from Peter Mitchell's field. The policeman came up and in a loud voice accused the laddie, while at the same time he threw in a hint or two that my lax discipline had something to do with the case.

"If they got a little mair o' the leather, things wud be different," he growled.

I do not like policemen; their little brief authority somehow manages to get my back up.

"What's the row?" I asked mildly.

"This young devil has been stealin' neeps," he roared, "and Mitchell's gaein' to mak a pollis court case o't."

I said nothing; I took Jimmy by the arm and walked towards the gate of Mitchell's field I vaulted it and deliberately pulled up a turnip and peeled it and ate it, while the constable stood writing down notes voluminously.

"Understand," I said to him, "that I am not primarily encouraging Jimmy to steal turnips; my one aim is to appear in the police court with him if he is charged. I would rather a thousand times be with him in the dock than with you and your farmer in the witness-box."

Peter Mitchell did not prosecute.

In these days Jimmy realised that he and I were friends; we understood each other. Now he does not think of trying to understand me; I am an ex-dominie, and that's enough for him. Macdonald is the real dominie; Jimmy must be circumspect when he is about else there will be ructions. I don't count: I have no authority. I should like to hear Macdonald's remarks to Jimmy if the constable came to the school to tell of one of the laddie's escapades.

I have lost Jimmy and a hundred others, but I thank heaven for the bairns left to me. They come up nearly every night, and they spend Saturdays and Sundays with me.

Last Saturday Macdonald came into the field where we were playing. Janet and the other girls froze at once; all the fun went out of them, and they looked at him timidly. He tried to show that he also could be playful and he tried to romp with them for a while. The romp wasn't a success; they were acting all the time, and when a girl "tigged" him she did so with a woefully apologetic air as if she would say: "Excuse my touching you, sir, but it's only a game, you know. I'll take care not to presume when we meet on Monday morning."

Luckily he did not stay long, and the girls resumed their attempt to tie my legs together with grass ropes, their motive being to stuff my mouth with brambles. I invited them down to the bothy for tea, and they rushed off to lay the table.

"And we'll look into a' yer drawers and places," cried Jean, "and read a' yer love-letters."

"If you could read I believe you *would* read them," I shouted after her.

"Eh! What an insult!" she cried. "Aw'll just go straucht doon to Maggie and tell her no to hae ye!"

After tea Gladys suddenly said: "Come on, we'll play at schules, eh?" The idea was hailed with delight, and Annie requisitioned the services of my new braces for a strap, and ranged us round the fire.

"Now," she said, "this is playtime and you are all outside, and when I blow the whistle you'll all come in."

"Blaw yer bugle," said Jean, "just to mak it like it was when ye were at the schule." So I played the "Fall In" and went out to play. I came in late.

"Why are you late?" demanded Annie.

I looked round the room vacantly.

"Yes!" I said with a nod of enlightenment.

The girls giggled, and Annie had to bite her lip to keep from laughing.

"Where have you been, sir?"

"Oh, no!" I cried, "at least I don't think so!"

Annie had to sit down and laugh.

"That's no fair," she said, "there shud be nae funnin' in the schule."

I sat down on the fender and pulled a face that Alfred Lester might have envied. Annie went into fits of laughter.

"Tell ye what, Annie," said Ellen, "we'll put the Mester oot, and we'll play oorsells," and I was dismissed the school. After deliberation they agreed to allow me to be an inspector provided I did not say anything.

When bairns play school they always put on the fine English. The teacher's main duty is to call erring pupils out and punish them.

"Now, Ellen Smith, what is two and two?"

"Four."

"Very good. Now we'll have an object lesson. What animal do we get milk from, Janet?"

"The cow."

"Very good. Now we'll have some geography. Where is the town of—?"

"Give us spellin' instead," cried Gladys.

"Come out, girl!" and Gladys was punished severely. Then Jean was punished for laughing.

"It's my chance o' bein' teacher noo," cried Ellen and Janet at the same time, and a treble scuffle for the strap followed. Janet got it.

"Now," she began, "I'll be Mister Macdonald. Put yer hands behind yer backs, and the first one that moves will hear about it!" They sat up like statues.

"Now, Jean Broon, you stand up and recite the *Elegy Written in a Country Churchyard*!" And Jean stood up and recited the first verse dramatically.

"That'll do. Sit down. Ellen Smith, I want you to say the first verse of Wordsworth's *Ode to the Imitations of Immorality*."

"P-Please, sir," tittered Gladys, "the inspector's laughin' like onything!"

I laughed immoderately, but it wasn't at Janet's malapropism that I laughed so much. I thought of Mrs. Wilks, the charwoman, who looked after the flat another man and I shared in Croydon. One morning she did not arrive to make the breakfast, and I went out to look for her. I found the old woman—she was sixty-three—standing at the foot of the stairs weeping.

"Great Scot!" I cried, "what's the matter?"

"My 'usband ain't goin' to allow me to char for you young gentlemen again."

"What for?" I asked in amazement.

"He . . . he accuses me of 'avin' immortal relations wiv you," she sobbed.

I hasten to add that her relations with us were not immortal: we sacked her a week later for pinching the cream.

"Sorry, Janet," I said at length, "proceed with your Imitations of Immorality, although personally I don't see the need for them; the real thing's good enough for me."

"Now," she said, "I'll be Mister Neill now."

Annie at once began to sing "Tipperary"; Ellen began to pull Gladys's hair; Jean pretended that she was biting a huge apple . . . and the teacher Janet took a cigarette from the box on the table and lit it.

"You gross libellers!" I cried, and I chased them out of the bothy.

* * * * *

To-night I had a long walk with Margaret. I tried to make her talk, for I want so much to know her views on things.

"You talk," she said; "I like to listen."

"But," I protested, "I'm always talking to you, and you listen all the time. I want to know what is in that wee head of yours . . . although I suppose that I ought to be satisfied with its exterior."

"You see," she said slowly and somewhat sadly, "I am not clever; I am only an ordinary farmer's daughter working in the dairy and the fields. If I told you what I was thinking you would not be interested."

We walked many yards in silence.

"It is all a mistake!" she suddenly burst out passionately. "I am not good enough for you, and when my bonny face is gone you will hate me. We have nothing in common, and if you met me in London you wouldn't be interested in me at all. You will bring clever women to the house and I—I will sit in a corner and say nothing, for I won't understand the things that you talk about. I am afraid to go to London with you."

"We'll stay here then," I said quietly.

"No!" she cried, "not that! I will stay here, but you must go to your work and your clever friends. O! it's all been a mistake!" She sat down on a fallen tree and wept silently. I sat down beside her and placed my arm round her shoulders.

"Margaret," I said softly, "we'll have a soul to soul talk about it. I'll tell you very very frankly what I think about the whole matter, and I'll try to deceive neither you nor myself.

"Intellectually you are not a soul-mate to me. That can't be possible seeing that you have never had the chance to develop your intellect. I know girls whose intellect is brilliant and whose sense of humour is delicious . . . but I don't love them. I like them; I love a witty conversation with them, but . . . I don't want to touch them. The touch of your hand sends a thrill through me, and there is no other hand in the world that can do that. I want to caress you, to hug you, to kiss your lips, to kiss your lovely neck. Margaret, I want you . . . and you are not my soul-mate. Margaret, I must have you.

"You see, dear, love is a thing that cannot be reasoned with. I once wrote down on paper a list of the qualities I wanted in the woman who should be my wife. She was to have blue eyes, a Grecian nose, auburn hair; she was to be tall and imperious; she was to be a fine pianist. Dear, your eyes are grey; your nose isn't Grecian; you aren't tall, and your limit as a pianist is *I'm a Little Pilgrim* played with one finger. You're hopeless, madam, but, dash it all!. . . I'll buy an auto-piano!

"According to all the rules I oughtn't to find any interest in you at all. Do you know that popular song *You Made Me Love You*? That's the only popular song I ever struck that has any philosophy in it. It has more real pathos in it than *The Rosary* and Tosti's *Goodbye* rolled into one.

"'You made me love you; I didn't want to do it,' . . . Margaret, that's the true story of love. Love is blind they say, but the truth is that love is mad. I didn't want to love you; my mind kept telling me that you were not the right woman . . . and here I sit in paradise because your head is on my shoulder. The whole thing's absurd and irrational. I almost believe that there is a real Cupid who fires his arrows broadcast; of course the little fellow is blind and he hits the wrong people."

I turned her face towards mine.

"Margaret, do you love me?"

"I love you," she whispered and she nestled more closely into my shoulder.

"And I love you," I replied, and kissed her brow. "It may be all a mistake, darling, but you and I are going to be man and wife."

"Anyway," I added, "we have no illusions about it. We've looked at the thing frankly and openly. We are blind, but we are going into it with our eyes open."

"You are getting silly again," laughed Margaret, and we forgot all our doubts and fears, and became two children playing with the toy we call love.

* * * * *

Margaret came to me to-night.

"Mr. Macdonald's evening school opens to-night. Do you think I should join it?"

"Why should you?" I asked.

"Oh, I have no education, and I want to learn things."

"Well," I said consideringly, "you'll learn things all right down there. You'll learn how to measure a field, and how to analyse a sentence; you'll learn a few things about the Stuart kings, and a few things about the British colonies. But, my dear, do you specially want to learn things like that?"

"I don't know what things I want to learn," she said sadly. "I think I want to know about the things you used to speak about at your evening school. Things that I don't agree with when you say them."

She laughed shortly.

"You know," she continued, "you used to make me angry sometimes. When you said that you didn't object to girls smoking I was wild with you. And I remember how shocked I was when you said that swearing navvies were no worse than we were. When you said that the text 'Children, obey your parents' gave bad advice I nearly got up and left the room."

"I expect that I *was* a sort of bombshell," I laughed.

"You made me think about things that I had never thought about before."

"That was what I was paid for, Margaret; I was educating you."

"What is education?" she asked.

"Education is thinking, Margaret. Most people take things for granted; they won't face truth. You don't like your sister Edith; she is catty and jealous. But you won't confess to yourself that you dislike Edith. All your training tells you that brotherly love is the accepted thing, and if you confessed to yourself that you are fonder of Jean Mackay than you are of Edith, you would think yourself a sinner of the worst type. If you want to be educated you must be ready to question everything; you must doubt everything. You must be very chary of making up your mind. Do you believe in ghosts?" I asked suddenly.

"Of course not!" she said with a smile. "Do you?"

"I don't know," I answered. "Lots of people claim to have seen them, and for that reason I leave the question open. There may not be ghosts, but I don't know enough about the subject to deny that they exist. I am quite ready to believe you if you tell me that you saw a ghost in the granary. I asked the question just to use it as an illustration. Popular opinion laughs at the idea of a ghost, but the thinking person won't accept the conventional view. Keep an open mind, Margaret, and believe when you are convinced.

"Education never stops; we are being educated every day of our lives. Why, only yesterday, I was up in the top field, and I heard a great squealing. I hurried to the place and was just in time to rescue a tiny rabbit from a weasel. I had seen a weasel kill a rabbit many a time before that, and I had never thought anything about it. But yesterday a sudden thought came to me. I remembered the words 'God is good,' and I began to think about them. Then I suddenly said to myself that the words were not true. The world is full of pain and terror; the great law of nature is: Eat or be eaten. I realised for the first time that every hedgerow is a horrid den of suffering and fear. Cruelty is Nature's name, Margaret."

"But," she cried in perplexity, "isn't there much good in the world too?"

"Yes, dear, there is much good in the world, but cruelty is much more powerful. You and I are cruel unthinkingly. We kill wasps before they sting us; we aren't good enough to give the poor brutes the benefit of the doubt. Your father is a very kind-hearted man, yet he never once thinks of the cruelty he perpetrates when he rears sheep and cattle and lambs for the butcher's knife. You and I dined on roast lamb often this summer, and we never thought of the poor wee creature's agony when the butcher cut its throat. Your mother is kind, yet she will kill a mouse without a thought, and the mouse is to me the bonniest creature that lives. Its great big glorious eyes fascinate me. Think of the kindly people who chase a poor half-starved fox with hounds and horses; sport is the cruellest thing in the world. Shooting, fishing, hunting . . . men are as cruel and as devilish as the tiger or the hawk, Margaret."

"Animals maybe don't feel the same as we do," she said.

"Don't you lay that flattering unction to your soul," I cried. "I used to believe that comforting tale of the scientist that the lower animals do not feel. I ceased to believe it when I tried to put a worm on a fish-hook. When I saw it wriggle about I said to myself: 'This is pain, or rather it is agony.' Think of the pain that your mares and cows suffer when they are having their young. You and I heard the screams of Polly when that dead foal was born this year.

"When you think of it, Margaret, man's chief end is not to glorify God as the Catechism says; his chief end is to eliminate pain . . . human pain. You have heard of vivisection? Performing operations on animals, often without chloroform. What's it all for? Not cruelty, as Bernard Shaw suggests; it's all done with the kindly purpose of finding out new ways to abolish human pain. Rabbits and guinea-pigs are dosed with all sorts of microbes so that scientists might discover how to protect human beings from the pain of disease. The doctors sometimes do manage to discover a new way to abolish a certain pain, and the pathetic thing is that while they torture animals to find a way to abolish pain a thousand scientists are busily engaged inventing weapons that will bring more pain into the world. It is an alarming thought that our doctors and nurses spend their lives trying to keep the unfit alive, while our armament makers spend their lives planning means to send the fit to their death. Lots of people have said that this war shows the failure of Christianity; what it really shows is the failure of Medicine. Medicine's primary aim is to keep people alive as long as possible; War's primary aim is to kill as many people as possible. War is really a battle between two branches of science, between shells and senna. The shell scientist won . . . and the medicine man buckled on a Sam Browne belt and went out to help his rival's victims. If the doctors of the world had realised that war was a defeat of their principles they would have gone on strike, and would no doubt have stopped the war by doing so. Every doctor should be a pacifist, but as a matter of fact very few doctors are pacifists."

"What is a pacifist?" asked Margaret.

"A pacifist is a man who loves peace so much that people look up almanacs to see whether his name was Schmidt a generation back, Margaret. He is usually a nervous man with the physical courage of a hen, but he has more moral courage than three army corps. He is usually a Conscientious Objector, and it takes the moral courage of a god to be that."

"They are just a lot of cowards!" cried Margaret with indignation.

"No," I said, "I can't agree with you. No coward will face the scorn of women and the contempt of men as these men do. Think of the life that lies in front of a

Conscientious Objector. Nobody will ever understand him; he will be an outcast for ever. Dear, it takes stupendous courage to put yourself in that position, and I can't think that any man could do it unless he were following principles that were dearer to him than the judgment of his fellow men. You see, Margaret, ordinary courage and moral courage are totally different things. I know a man who won the V.C. for a very brave deed, and that chap wouldn't wear a made-up tie for all the decorations in the world; he wouldn't have the moral courage to be seen walking down the street with a Bengali. The more imagination you have the higher is your moral courage, but imagination is fatal to physical courage. Moral courage belongs to the thinker; physical courage to the doer. And I can't help thinking that moral courage goes with unhealthiness. I am quite sure that physical courage is primarily dependent on physical health. If my liver is out of order I tremble to open a letter; I can't walk ten yards in the dark; and the arrival of a telegram would give me a fainting fit. Nerves are always unhealthy, and as thinkers are always highly strung people I conclude that thinking is unhealthy. Thinkers are mad, Margaret, mad as hatters."

"Mad!"

"Yes. The lunatic is merely the man whose brain is different from the brain of the average man. The average man does not imagine himself to be Jesus Christ, and when a man does imagine himself to be Christ we say that he is mad, and we shut him up. He may be a Christ for all we know. I don't know why the community didn't shut up Shaw when he first preached that obedience was one of the Seven Deadly Virtues. The average man didn't agree with him, and we can say that Shaw is therefore mad. You see, dear, man is firstly an animal; Joe Smith the butcher down in the village is an animal, a fine healthy animal. He is primitive man, and thinking is the last thing he could attempt. Thinking is an acquired characteristic; it isn't a natural thing, and anything unnatural is diseased. A thinker is as much a freak as a man born with two heads. And that's why I say that thinkers are unhealthy. Blake the great poet was mad; Ibsen the great Norwegian dramatist died in the mad-house; Shelley was diseased; Milton was blind, Keats a consumptive; nearly every great composer of music who ever lived was mad."

"But," laughed Margaret, "you said that education was thinking, and now you say that thinkers are all mad."

"Yes, but madness is what the world needs. All these villagers down there are absolutely sane, but the world won't be a scrap the better for their existence. I prefer a world of Shelleys and Ibsens to a world of Jack Johnsons and Sandows . . . and Joe Smiths. A great German philosopher called Nietzsche preached the gospel of Superman. He wanted a fine race of powerful men who would rule the world. Some people say that Napoleon and Cæsar and Cromwell were Supermen, but the real Supermen were men like Christ and Ibsen and Darwin and Shelley; a fighter is a nobody, but a man with a message is a Superman."

"I don't understand," said Margaret dully; "what do you mean by having a message?"

"A messenger is a man who forces people to consider things that they wouldn't consider without being prompted. Christ's message was love; He encouraged men to act according to the good that was in them; the kindliness, the charity, the love. And the fact that shooting and hunting and lamb eating still persist shows that we pay but little attention to Christ's message. Shelley's message was freedom, freedom to think and to live one's own life. You'll find that there are only the two kinds of message . . . love and freedom."

"The evangelists who were holding meetings in the school last winter used to speak about their 'message,'" said Margaret. "Would you say that they were Supermen?"

"They were Superwomen," I said hastily. "They depended on emotionalism. They said nothing new, and they would refuse to consider anything new if you asked them to. They had no power to think; they quoted all the time. Consequently their message evaporated; when the magnetism of their appeal went away the converts lapsed into their old sinful ways. They didn't understand the message they tried to deliver; they had never really thought out Christ's philosophy. They had got hold of a catch phrase or two, and they kept shouting: 'Though your sins be as scarlet they shall be made whiter than snow.' But I am quite sure that they did not know what they meant by sin. Christ's chief message was: 'Love one another,' but they made it out to be: 'Love yourself so well that you may cry for salvation from the wrath to come.'"

Margaret looked at the clock on my mantelpiece.

"O!" she cried, "it's eight o'clock . . . and the class began at seven! I can't go now."

At the door she paused for a moment; then she came back slowly.

"I won't attend his class," she said thoughtfully; "I think I'll just come over to see you every night, and you'll talk to me and educate me."

"Well," I smiled, "I will give you a wider education than Macdonald can give you. For example . . . this!"

"I could get any amount of teaching in kissing," she tittered.

"Possibly, darling . . . but there is no teacher hereabouts with my knowledge and experience of the art."

"You horrid pig!" she laughed, and she pulled my hair.

CHAPTER XIV.

Janet and Annie came up to me to-night. "Hullo!" I cried, "what's become of Ellen and Gladys and Jean?"

"We're no speakin' to them," said Annie loftily.

"Cheeky things!" said Janet with scorn.

I became interested at once.

"Rivals in a love affair?" I asked.

They sniffed, and ignored the query.

"It was Jean," said Annie bitterly. "She went and telt the Mester that Aw spoke when he was oot o' the room."

"Aye," said Janet, "she put doon my name tae. Wait er I get her at hame the nicht!"

I understood. Macdonald evidently favours the obnoxious practice of setting a bairn to spy on the others . . . a silly thing to do.

"Aye," went on Annie, "and she called us navvies' lasses!"

"And you replied?"

"Aw telt her to g'wa hame and darn the hole in her stockin'. 'Aye,' Aw said, 'and ye can wash yer neck at the same time, Jean Broon!'"

"But," I said, "Jean never has a dirty neck, Annie."

"Weel, what did she say that Aw was a navvy's lass for then?" she demanded indignantly.

"I'm afraid that she has seen you speaking to navvies, Annie."

Annie became excited. She clutched Janet by the sleeve.

"Eh! What an insult!" she cried. "Janet Broon, div Aw speak to navvies?"

"Never in a' yer life," said Janet firmly, "never wance . . . unless yon day that the twa o' them speered at ye the wye to the huts."

"But Aw didna answer," said Annie quickly; "Aw just pointed."

"Are you sure?" I asked.

"Sure as daith," she declared solemnly, and she cut her breath. "Aw maybe wud ha' spoken," she admitted, "but Aw had a muckle lump o' jaw-stickin' toffee in my mooth, and Aw cudna speak supposin' Aw had wanted to."

"Pointing was as bad as speaking," I said.

"If it was," said Annie tensely, "Jean never washes her neck. So there!"

They departed, and in half-an-hour the enemy came up. They sat in the bothy in silence for a time.

"Well," I said cheerily, "what's the news to-night?"

"We're fechtin'," said Gladys, "fechtin' wi' Annie and Janet."

"What's it all about, eh?"

"The Mester gar me write doon the names o' them that was speakin'," blurted out Jean, "and Aw put doon their names."

"Yes," chimed in Ellen, "and syne they ca'ed Jean a tramp, and said that the Mester gae her the job o' writin' doon the names cos she was sic a bad writer and needed practice."

"Aye," said Gladys, "and they telt me my mither got my pink frock dyed black when my faither deed."

"And it wasna her pink frock," cried Ellen; "it was her green ane."

"This is alarming," I said with concern. "But tell me, Jean, did you say anything to them?"

"Aw never said a word!"

"Not one word?"

"They cried to us that we was navvies' dochters, and Aw just said: 'Aw wud rather be a navvy's dochter than the dochter o' Annie Miller's faither onywye.'"

"They telt Jean to wash her neck," said Gladys.

Jean smiled grimly.

"Aye, but they got mair than they bargained for! I just says to them, Aw says: 'Annie Miller, gang hame and tell yer faither to redd up his farm-yaird. Aye, and tell yer mither to wash yer heid ilka week instead o' twice a year!'"

"But," I protested, "Annie gets her hair washed every Saturday night!"

"And Aw get my neck washen ilka mornin'!"

"All right, Jean, but you haven't told me what you said to Janet."

"Jan! I soon settled her! I just says to her says Aw: 'Wha stailt the plums that mither brocht hame on Saturday nicht?'"

"And did Jan steal the plums?" I asked.

"She did that!"

"And you never touched them?"

"No the plums," she said frankly; "Aw wasna sic a thief as that. Aw only took a wee corner o' the fig toffee."

I scratched my head thoughtfully.

"This is a bonny racket, girls. I don't know what to make of it. I think you'll better make it up."

"Never!" cried Jean stoutly. "Ellen and Gladys and me's never to speak to them again; are'n we no, Ellen?"

"Never!" cried Ellen.

"No if they were to gang doon on their bended knees!" declared Gladys.

"That's awkward for you, Jean," I said. "Do you mean to tell me that you won't speak to Jan when you are sleeping together?"

"Aw'll just gie her a dig in the ribs wi' my elbow to mak her lie ower, but Aw'll no open my mooth."

"And what if your mother says to you: 'Jean, tell Janet to feed the hens?'"

"Aw'll just hand her the corn-dish and point to the henhoose."

"And put oot my tongue at her," she added.

"Jean," I said suddenly, "I'll bet you a shilling that you are speaking to Jan and Annie by to-morrow night at four."

"Aw dinna hae a shillin'," she said ruefully, "but Aw bet ye a hapenny Aw'm no!"

* * * * *

To-night Jean came running up to me when school was dismissed.

"Gie's my hapenny!" she cried; "Aw didna speak to Annie and Janet a' day!"

"Honest?"

"It's true," said Ellen, "isn't it Gladys?"

"Then I'll pay up my debt of honour," I said, and I held out a ha'penny.

Jean took it, and then she set off round the steading in great haste. She returned with her arms round Janet and Annie.

"Aw got Bets Burnett to tell them aboot the ha'penny," she confessed, "and to speer them no to speak to me a' day and Aw wud gie them a bit o' sugarelly."

"You scheming besom!" I cried and I laid her on my bothy table and sat on her.

"Eh! Jean!" said Gladys, "if only ye had said ye wud bet a shillin'!"

"Dear me," I said hastily, "when I come to think of it I did bet a shilling. Jean bet a hapenny, but I distinctly remember saying that I was betting a shilling. Here you are, Jean!" but Jean refused it with indignation. Not one of them would touch it.

"Right!" I cried. "I'm going down to get cigarettes. Who's coming?"

I spent a shilling on sweets and chocolate. No one would accept a single sweetie.

"I'll give myself toothache if I eat them," I said. They paid no heed.

"I won't invite one of you to my marriage if you don't take them." They wavered, but did not give way.

"All right," I said with an air of great determination, "here goes!" and I tossed the bag into the field. They made no sign of interest, and we walked up the brae. Jim Jackson was coming down with his milk.

"Jim," I began, "if you go down to that first gate, and look over the hedge you'll find—"

I got no farther.

"Come on!" cried Janet, "Aw dinna want them, but Jim Jackson's no to get them onywye!"

I was glad to note that they gave Jim a handful as he passed.

* * * * *

To-day was fair day, and the bairns all went to town. I cycled in in the afternoon, and took the girls on the hobby-horses. I also stood Jim Jackson and Dickie Gibson into the stirring drama entitled: "The Moaning Spirit of the Moat . . . a Drama of the Supernatural." I had a few shies at the hairy-dolls, and won two cocoanuts and a gold tie-pin. Then I stood fascinated by the style of the gentleman who kept the ring stall. Several articles were hung from hooks, and you tried to throw a ring on to a hook. His invariable comment on a ploughman's attempt was: "Hard luck for the alarum-clock! Give the gentleman a collar-stud."

About five o'clock Jim came up to me.

"How now, duke," I said breezily, "how much money have you left?"

I was astonished to hear that he had half-a-crown.

"Why!" I cried, "you told me at three o'clock that you had only ninepence left!"

He smiled enigmatically.

"Aw've been speculatin'," he said proudly. "Have ye seen the mannie that's sellin' watches and things at the Cross? Aw was standin' there wi' Geordie Steel this mornin', and the mannie speered if onybody wud gie him a penny for a shillin', and naebody wud dae it at first. Syne a ploughman gae him a penny and he got the shillin'. Syne the mannie speers again, and Geordie got a shillin' for a ha'penny. Syne he began to sell watches, and the first man that bocht a watch got his money back. Syne he held up a gold chain, and the man that bocht that he got his money back. Syne he held up anither gold chain and said he wud sell it for half-a-crown. So Geordie ups and hauds oot his half-croon, and it was a' the money he had. Weel, he gets the chain, but no his money back. 'Don't go away,' says the mannie; 'each and every man as buys an article of jewellery will have his reward.'

"Weel, Aw waited for half-an-hoor, but Geordie hadna got onything by that time, so Aw goes and sees the boxin' show. After that Aw had a shot o' the shoagin' boats, and syne Aw went back to the Cross. Geordie was ay waitin' for his reward. So Aw says to him: 'He's likely forgot a' aboot it, Geordie; tell him!' So Geordie hauds up his gold chain and says: 'Hi, mannie, ye said Aw was to get a reward!' 'O, yes,' says the mannie, 'and so you shall! I want you to keep these eighteen carat gold sleeve-links as a memento of this occasion,' and he shoved a pair o' links into Geordie's hands. After that he shut his box and said he wud hae anither sale at four punctual.

"Weel, Aw began to think aboot the thing, and when he began again he did the same thing. 'Will anyone oblige me by giving me a penny for half-a-crown?' he says, and Aw was just puttin' up my hand when a man held up his penny. 'Hi!' I cried, 'Aw'll gie ye tuppence if ye like!' and the mannie that was selling the things he lauched and handed me the half-croon. 'You're the kind of lad I'm looking for for an apprentice,' he says, but whenever Aw got the money Aw turned and ran awa, and he cries after me: 'Yes, you are the lad I want, but I see you are too clever for me.'"

I asked Jim to show me the half-crown, and I examined it. It was quite genuine, but I said to Jim: "Men like that usually give away bad money." He was off like a flash, and when he came back he carried twenty-five pennies and ten hapennies.

"If he starts to sell again," he announced, "Aw'll get Geordie to hand up the penny, but Aw'll no stand aside him."

The girls each brought my "market" to me to-night . . . a packet of rock. I asked about their spendings. Janet had bought three lucky-bags and nine lucky eggs. She had had no luck, and was somewhat grieved at the fact that Jean had bought only one lucky-egg and had got a new hapenny in it. Janet would have bought another egg with the hapenny, but I was not surprised to hear that Jean had bought sugarelly. Ellen had bought a tupenny note-book and a copying-ink pencil, a rubber and a card of assorted pen-nibs. Gladys had spent her all on lemon-kailie, the heavenly powder you get in oval boxes, with two wee tin spoons to sup it with.

Jim came up later. His pockets contained three trumps, or Jewish harps as they are called in catalogues, three copying-ink pencils, a pencil that wrote red at one end and blue at the other, two mouth-organs, a wire puzzle, and . . . Geordie's gold chain. The latter he had bought for tuppence and a double-stringed trump.

"Aw spent three and fowerpence," he said, "but dinna tell the Mester!"

"Why not, Jim?"

"Cos he'll be angry. He told us yesterday no to spend oor money at the market, but to bring it and put it in the Savin's Bank."

I wonder what becomes of the money that children put into the Savings Bank. I think that their parents usually collar it at some time or another. I half suspect that quite a number of cottage pianos owe their appearance to the children's bank-books. I stopped the saving business when I was down in the school. Bairns seldom get money, and sugarelly is like Robinson Crusoe: you must tackle it when you are young, or you never enjoy it thoroughly. I think it cruel to make a bairn bank the penny it gets for running a message. Spending is always a pleasant thing, but a bairn gets more delirious joy out of buying a hapenny lucky-bag than an adult gets out of buying a thousand guinea Rolls Royce motor.

Some parents are foolish enough to give their bairns too much to spend. Little Mary Wallace has a penny every day of the year. I think that foolish of her mother. Spending must be a very rare thing if it is to yield the highest pleasure.

I would advise bairns to save when they have a definite object in view. To lay up treasure in the Post Office Savings Bank is, for a bairn, about as tempting as laying up treasure in heaven. Bairns can't entertain remote possibilities. You can tell a boy that a sum in the bank will help him to buy clothes or a bicycle when he is a man, and the prospect does not thrill him. You can't persuade a boy to cast his eyes on the years to come when his eyes are rivetted on a cake of chewing-gum in the village shop window. If he saves it should be for a direct tangible object. He takes up a Gamage catalogue (the most delightful of books to a boy), and he sees an illustration of a water-pistol costing a shilling. If he is a boy of spirit he will deny himself sweeties for a month in order to get that pistol. The self-discipline necessary to enable a village boy to buy a water-pistol will do him infinitely more good than all the discipline of all the Macdonalds in Scotland. I would have all children poor in money, but I would give them the opportunity of earning enough money to buy their toys. A little poverty is good for anybody; I would recommend a young man to live on twelve shillings a week for a year or two; he would begin to see things in proportion.

A friend of mine bases his antipathy to Socialism on this view of poverty. He argues that poverty brings out self-reliance, pluck, grit. When I ask him why he doesn't support Socialism as a means of bringing all these advantages to the poor wealthy folk, he is at a loss. In a manner I agree with him; poverty will often give a race splendid characteristics. But Socialism recognises that the wealth of the world is divided most unequally. At one end you have luxury that makes men degenerate; at the other end you have poverty that makes men swine. If Shaw's idea of equal incomes could be carried out each person would be in the position of a member of the present lower middle class; he would be rich enough to be well-fed and happy, and he would be poor enough to discipline himself to make sacrifices to attain an object. I don't think that any man should satisfy more than one desire at a time. If Andrew Carnegie wants a motor-car and a four manual organ he has simply to tell his secretary to write out two cheques. But if I want a motor-cycle and an Angelus player-piano I've got to give up one desire. I know that I'll tire of either, and all I have to do is to sit down and wonder which novelty will last the longer. I want both very much. A 2¾-h.p. Douglas would be delightful, and an Angelus with lots of rolls would charm the long nights away. But . . . there is Margaret. I begin to think of blankets and sheets and pots and pans. I don't want any of these plebeian articles, but I want Margaret very much, and I know that along with her I must take the whole bunch of kitchen utensils.

I begin to feel sorry for millionaires. One of the finer pleasures of life is the desiring of a thing you can't buy. The sorriest man in story is the millionaire who arrived at a big hotel very late, so late that he couldn't be served with supper. He straightway sent for the proprietor and asked the price of the hotel. He wrote out a cheque on the spot . . . and called for his sausage and mashed—or whatever the dish was. No wonder that millionaires complain of indigestion.

That story contains a fine moral. I don't exactly know what the moral is, but I hazard the opinion that the moral is this:—Never buy a hotel in order to get a plate of sausage and mashed. Millionaires might be defined as men who buy hotels in order to get sausage and mashed . . . and they can't digest the sausage when they have got it. When a Carnegie builds a great organ in a great hall he is really buying the whole hotel. He is taking an unfair advantage of his fellow music-lovers. A plate of sausage and mashed would be of far greater moment to G. K. Chesterton than to the millionaire, but G. K. couldn't buy the whole hotel; he would merely swear volubly and tighten the belt of his waistcoat . . . if that were possible. The millionaire should not have this advantage over Chesterton. So a millionaire should not have any advantage over a music-lover. Collinson, the Edinburgh University organist, has no doubt a greater appreciation of organ music than a Carnegie, but he has to go down to his church organ on a winter night if he wants to play a Bach fugue. Money is power, they say, but money is worse than power; it is tyranny. A successful pork-merchant whose one talent is his ability to tell at a glance how much pig it takes to fill a thousand tins of lamb cutlet, may buy up half the treasures of the world if he likes. Priceless pictures and violins lie in millionaires' halls, while students of genius study prints and practise on two guinea fiddles. At first sight this seems a problem that Horatio Bottomley would handle eagerly and popularly, but the problem is really a deep one. When humanity abolishes the power to amass millions who is to have the priceless treasures? In the case of art the community of course. (I see in to-day's paper that Rodin has bequeathed all his works to France.) But what of the Stradivarius violins? I would have them lent to the geniuses. Who is to decide who the geniuses are? That is a question of fundamentals, and if I had left the question to Mr. Bottomley I think he would have recommended his readers to "write to John Bull about it."

I begin to feel that I am talking through my hat as the vulgar phrase has it. My baccy's finished, and I can't concentrate my attention on any subject. What I meant to do was to show that a millionaire is a man to be pitied. To buy a Titian painting when your tastes lie in the direction of Heath Robinson's *Frightful War Pictures* is as pathetic a thing to do as to sit out a classical concert when your tastes lead you to a passionate love for ragtime. And buying a Titian is a simple case of buying the hotel in order to get the sausage and mashed that you can't eat.

Millionaires . . . no, it's no good; I'll have to fold up my typewriter till I get some more baccy.

CHAPTER XV.

Margaret was reading a few pages of my diary to-night.

"Why," she said, "it's all about yourself!"

"Not all," I said hastily, "some of it is about you . . . but I won't let you read that part until you are my wife. If you knew the terrible things I have written about you you would go off straightway and marry Joe Smith."

"You think quite a lot of yourself," she said with a laugh.

"Everybody thinks a lot of himself, Margaret. If I died to-night you would probably have forgotten the shape of my nose by the time you were sixty, but you'll never forget that I told you your neck was the loveliest neck in the county. My old grandmother used to tell me again and again of the man who stopped her on the road when she was seven and told her that her eyes were like blue stars. His name was Donald Gunn . . . but she could never recollect the names of the girls she played with.

"The people who don't think much of themselves are people who have no personality to be proud of . . . personally I haven't yet met any of the brand. We all have something that we're conceited about, dear. You are conceited about your eyes and your neck and your hair. Jean Hardie is about the plainest girl in the village, but I could bet that she thinks her hair the most glorious in the place . . . and it is too.

"Very often we are conceited about the things that we can do worst. I can draw pretty well, but I'm not conceited about it. I can't sing for nuts . . . and if anyone left the room when I was warbling I should hate him to all eternity. I like a man to be an egotist . . . if he has got an ego of any value. Peter MacMannish is a type of egotist that should be put into a lethal chamber. He has no ego to talk about, but he imagines that his stomach is his ego, and he will talk to you for an hour about the 'yirkin" of the organ in question."

"What is an ego?" asked Margaret. "I never heard the word before."

"It is the Latin word for 'I,' and a person who uses the pronoun 'I' very often is called an egotist. The other word egoist has a different meaning; it means a person who thinks of himself all the time, a selfish person. You can be an egotist without being an egoist, and vice versa. Peter Mitchell never talks about himself; while you talk about yourself he is thinking out a method of selling you something at double its value.

"There are two kinds of egotist . . . the man who talks about what he does, and the man who talks about what he thinks. When I get letters from my friends they are full of "I's." Dorothy Westbrook, a college friend of mine, a medallist in half-a-dozen classes, fills eight pages with small talk.... 'I went to see Tree in the Darling of the Gods last night,' and so on. I generally skip the eight pages and look at the post-script. May Baxter, another college friend, a girl who wouldn't recognise a medal if you showed her one, writes ten pages, and she usually commences with something like this:—'I was re-reading *The New Machiavelli* last night, and I think that I begin to despise Wells now.' I read her letter a dozen times. When she does take a fancy for the other kind of egotism she is delightful: she doesn't tell me what she does; she tells me what she is.

"I have half a mind to leave you for a year, Margaret, just to give you a chance of writing about yourself. I won't be able to write to you in the same strain: I wrote myself out when I fell in love at twenty-two. You can only be a good letter-writer once, and that is when you are discovering yourself for the first time, and ramming it down on paper as fast as you can. I used to write letters of twenty foolscap pages, but now I never write a letter if I can help it. Life has lost most of its glamour when you realise that you have discovered yourself. It's a sad business discovering yourself, dear. You set out to persuade yourself that you are a genius or a saint, and, after a long examination of yourself you discover that you are a sorry creature. You set out with Faith and Hope at your elbow, and at the end you find that they have long since left you, but you find that Charity has taken their place. Charity begins at home says the proverb, and I take this to mean that Charity comes to you when you find yourself at home, when you discover yourself. I used to be the most uncharitable of mortals, but now I seldom judge a man or woman. Peter MacMannish gets drunk; I do not condemn him, for I have looked on the wine when it was red. Mary MacWinnie has had two illegitimate children; I am a theoretical Don Juan. Shepherd, the rabbit-catcher, has an atrocious temper; I do not judge him, because, although my own temper is pretty equable, I can realise that the man can no more help his temper than I can the size of my feet. Charity comes to you when you have discovered how weak you are, and that's what kept me from being a good code teacher. I was such a poor weak devil that I couldn't bring myself to make the boys salute me or fear me."

"You say that, but you don't believe it."

"I believe it, Margaret. My whole theory of education is built on my abject humility. My chief objection to Macdonald is that he ignores his own weaknesses. He has never analysed himself to see what manner of man he is. If he could look into his heart and discover all the little meanesses and follies and hypocrisies he would not have the courage to make a boy salute him; he would not have the impudence to strap a boy for swearing. One of the worst things about Macdonald and a thousand other dominies is that they have forgotten their childhood. A dominie should never grow up. I would take away from all students their text-books on School Management and Psychology, and put into their hands Barrie's *Peter Pan* and Stevenson's *A Child's Garden of Verses*.

"Margaret, why can't people see that the Macdonald system is all wrong? What in all the world is the use of dominies and ministers and parents posing before children? What is respect but a pose? What is Macdonald's sternness but a pose? He is a kindly decent fellow outside his school. The bairns meet with pose the first thing in the morning when they enter the school. They stand up and repeat the Lord's Prayer monotonously, and without the faintest realisation of what they are saying. The dominie closes his eyes and clasps his hands in front of him, and I don't believe there is a single dominie in Scotland who really prays each morning. For that matter I don't believe that there are half-a-dozen ministers who repeat the prayer on Sundays with any thought of its meaning. The morning prayer is a gigantic sham. When I said to Macdonald that I would have it abolished in schools he almost had a fit. The bigger the sham is the louder is the screaming in its defence if you attack it.

"Think of all the shams that parents practise. They pretend that babies come in the doctor's pocket; they pretend that a lie is as much an abomination to them as it is to the Lord; they imply by their actions that they never stole apples in their lives; they hint that they don't know what bad language means. They live a life that is one continuous lie."

"I don't understand that," said Margaret with a puzzled look.

"A mother lies to her child when she tells it that it is wicked when it makes a noise; a father lies to his son when he tells him that he will come to a bad end if he smokes any more cigarettes. Worse than that they lie by negation. The father changes his 'Hell!' into 'Hades!' when he hits his thumb with a hammer; the mother says 'Tut Tut!' when she means 'Damnation!' Both go to church as an example to their offspring . . . and going to church is in most cases a lie. Nearly every father of a family says grace before meat, and he generally delays the practice until his first-born is old enough to take notice. Then there is the lie about relationship. A child never discovers that its father has about as much love for its mother's aunt as he has for the King of Siam.

"Convention is one huge lie, Margaret. You lift your hat when a coffin goes by; you beg my pardon when I ask you to pass the marmalade; you stand bare-headed when a band plays the National Anthem. It's all a lie, dear, a pretty lie perhaps, but a lie all the same. But after all, the manners business is a minor affair; you can't abolish it, and if you try you will only make yourself ridiculous. But the other lies, the hypocritical lies that are told to children . . . these are dangerous. An ardent republican will doff his hat when the band plays *God Save the King*, and be none the worse; the unpleasantness that might follow his keeping his hat on his head wouldn't be worth it. But if I pretend to a child that I am above human frailty I am doing a hellish thing that may have devilish consequences."

"Your language is awful!" cried Margaret in feigned protest.

"I was quoting *The Ancient Mariner*, dear; you read it at my evening class, and you have evidently forgotten it. Since the beginning of humanity children have been warped by the attitudinising of their elders. A child is imitative always; he hasn't the power to think out biggish things for himself. He is tremendously docile; he will believe almost anything you tell him, and he will accept an older person's pose without question. If one of the village boys were to see Macdonald stotting home drunk he would be like the countryman who, when he saw a giraffe for the first time, cried: 'Hell!. . . I don't believe it!' And the sad thing is that they never are able to distinguish between pose and truth. The villagers who used to tell my bairns that I was daft don't realise what pose is; they have never found the right values. When they criticise the minister or the dominie they invariably fasten on the wrong things. They are beginning to criticise Macdonald because he insists on a bairn's bringing a written excuse when he has been absent, but they believe in all his poses—his love for respect, his authority, his whackings, his hiding of his pipe when a child is near, his passion for sex morality, his dignity, his . . . his frayed frock coat that he wears in school."

"The poor man's only wearing out his old Sunday coat!" protested Margaret.

"I never thought of that, Margaret; I'll cut out the coat. But he shouldn't have a frock coat anyway. When we get married I shall insist on dressing in an old golfing jacket, flannel bags, and a soft collar. The only danger is that men of my stamp are apt to make unconvention conventional. It's a very difficult thing to keep from posing when you are protesting against pose."

"Oh! I don't understand the half of what you say," said Margaret wearily.

"That means that you think my lips might be better employed, you schemer!" and I . . . well, I don't think I need write everything down after all.

* * * * *

"There was a venter locust at the schule the day," remarked Annie. I was brushing my boots at the bothy door, and the girls sat on the step and watched me.

"A what?" I asked.

"A venter locust. Ye paid a penny to get in, and Jim Jackson gaithered the pennies in the mannie's hat and got in for nothing, for he didna put his ain penny in."

"What sort of show was it, Annie?"

"He had a muckle doll wi' an awfu' ugly face, and he asked it questions."

"Did it answer them?"

"Aye. It opened its great big mooth."

"There maybe was a gramaphone inside," suggested Gladys.

"Jim Jackson said that it was the mannie that was speakin' a' the time," said Janet.

"Jim Jackson was bletherin'," said Annie with scorn. "Aw watched 'im, and his mooth never moved a' the time."

"Perhaps he was talking through his hat, Annie," I said.

"He wasna," she cried, "for his hat was on the Mester's desk fu' o' pennies!"

"Well," I ventured, "the proverb says that money talks, you know."

"Weel," tittered Annie, "there wasna much money to talk, for the pennies was nearly a' hapennies!"

"Aw dinna understand how that doll managed to speak," said Ellen, and I proceeded to explain the mysteries of ventriloquism to them. Then I told them my one ventriloquist yarn.

A broken-down ventriloquist stopped at a village inn one hot day, and stared longingly through the bar door. He hadn't a cent in his pocket. He sat down on the bench and gazed wearily at a stray mongrel dog that had followed him for days. Suddenly inspiration came to him. He rose and walked into the bar.

"A pint of beer, mister!" he cried, and pretended to fumble for his money, when the landlord placed the tankard on the bar counter.

The dog looked up into his face.

"Here, mister," said the dog, "ain't I going to get one?"

The landlord started.

"That's a remarkable animal," he said with staring eyes.

"Pretty smart," said the ventriloquist indifferently.

"I'll—I'll buy that dog," said the landlord eagerly; "I'll give you five pounds for him."

The ventriloquist considered for a while.

"All right," he said at length, "I hate to part with an old friend like him, but I must live, and I have no money."

The landlord counted out the five sovereigns, and the ventriloquist drank up his beer and made for the door.

"Better come round and take hold of the dog," he said, "or he'll follow me."

The landlord lifted the bar-flap and took hold of the dog by the collar.

At the door the ventriloquist looked back. The dog gazed at him.

"You brute," it cried, "you've sold me for vulgar gold. I swear that I'll never speak again."

I paused.

"And, you know, girls, he never did."

"Eh," cried Janet, "what a shame! The public-hoose mannie wud leather the puir beast to mak' it speak."

"That's the real point of the story, Jan. A story is no good unless it leaves something to the imagination."

"The Mester gae us a story to write for composition the day," said Annie. "It was aboot a boy that was after a job and a' the boys were lined up and they had to go in to see the man, and he had a Bible lyin' on the floor, and a' the lads steppit over it, but this laddie he pickit it up and got the job."

"That's what you call a story with a moral, Annie. It is meant to teach you a lesson. The best stories have no morals . . . neither have the people who listen to them."

"We had to write the story," said Ellen, "and syne we had to tell why the boy got the job. Aw said it was becos he was a guid boy and went to the Sunday Schule."

"Aw said it was becos he was a pernikity sort o' laddie that liked things to be tidy," said Gladys.

Annie laughed.

"Aw said the man was maybe a fat man that cudna bend doon to pick it up. What did you say, Jan?"

"Aw dinna mind," said Janet ruefully, "but when the Mester cried me oot for speakin', Aw picked up a geography book on the floor, just to mak the Mester think that Aw had learned a lesson frae his story, but he gae me a slap on the lug for wastin' time comin' oot."

"Jim Jackson got three scuds wi' the strap for his story," said Annie.

"Ah!" I cried, "what did he write?"

"He said that the laddie maybe hadna a hankie, and his nose was needin' dichted and he didna like to let the man see him dichtin' it wi' the sleeve o' his jaicket, so he bent doon to pick up the Bible and dicht his nose on the sly at the same time."

"Yes," I said sadly, "that's Jim Jacksonese, pure and simple. Poor lad!"

"The Mester said he was a vulgar fellow," said Janet.

"A low-minded something or other, he ca'ed him," said Gladys.

"But he didna greet when he got the strap," said Annie, "he just sniffed thro' his nose and—and dichted it wi' his sleeve."

I knew then that all the Macdonalds in creation couldn't conquer my Jim.

CHAPTER XVI.

Macdonald and I were comparing notes to-night.

"I found that Monday was always a noisy day in school," I said; "the bairns were always unsettled."

"I don't find that," he said; "Friday is their worst day. I don't understand that."

"Friday was my free day," I said.

"What do you mean by free day?"

"Every bairn did what it liked."

"Good Lord!" exclaimed Macdonald.

"That's nothing," I laughed, "why, I gave them a free week once."

"What was your idea. Laziness?"

"Laziness! My dear boy, I never put in such a hard week in my life. A boy would come out and ask for a certain kind of sum, then a girl would bring out a writing book and ask for a setting; by the time I had attended to these, a dozen were waiting."

"Did they all work?"

"They were all active. Dickie Gibson spent the week in sketching; Geordie Steel read five penny dreadfuls; Janet Brown played at anagrams; Annie Miller read *The Weekly Welcome*; Ellen Smith worked arithmetic all week and Jock Miller wrote a novel. Jock spent half his dinner-hour writing."

"That's what a school should be," I added.

"Ah! So you think that reading penny dreadfuls is education?"

"Everything you do is education."

"So you say, but I want to know the exact educational value of penny dreadfuls. My idea is that they do boys harm."

"That's what the magistrates say, Macdonald. They trace all juvenile crime to penny dreadfuls and the cinema. The British have a passion for scapegoats. We have war with Germany. 'Who did this?' demand the public indignantly. 'Who's going to be whopped for this?' They look round and Haldane's rotund figure catches their eye. Haldane becomes the scapegoat. So with poor Birrell when the Sinn Fein rebellion occurred. So the magistrates fasten on the poor penny dreadful and the picture-film. Obviously they do so because they are too stupid to think out the problem of crime. Picture-houses have about as much to do with crime as Birrell had to do with the dissatisfaction in Ireland."

"Come, come," said Macdonald impatiently, "keep to the point: what educational value has the penny dreadful?"

"The educational value that any reading matter has. It doesn't give you many ideas, but you can say the same thing about Barrie's novels or Kipling's. It gives a boy a vocabulary and it exercises his imagination."

"Wouldn't he be better reading good literature? Dickens for instance?"

"I don't see it," I said; "he isn't ripe enough to understand Dickens's humour, and for a boy I should say Dickens is bad. His style is grandiose and stilted, his periphrasis is the most delightful in the world to an educated person, but it is bad for a child. About half of *David Copperfield* is circumlocution, but a boy should learn to speak and write boldly. The penny dreadful goes straight to the point. 'Harold looked straight into the blue barrel of a Colt automatic.' Translate that into Dickensese (an ugly word to coin, I admit) and you have something like this:—'Harold contemplated with extreme apprehension the circular muzzle of a Cerulean blue automatic pistol of the kind specifically manufactured by the celebrated world-famous American firm of Colt.'"

"Poor Dickens," laughed Macdonald.

"But you see my point?" I persisted. "Circumlocution is a Victorian nuisance. Any man who has anything to say says it simply and without trappings. And, mind you, Macdonald, people who use circumlocution in style use it in thought. The average man loves flowery literature, and he loves flowery thoughts. The contest between the plain style and the aureate style is really the old contest between realism and romance. The romantic way to look at crime is to fix your attention on drink and penny dreadfuls and cinema shows; the realistic way is to look bravely at the economic division of wealth that causes poverty and disease, the father and mother of crime."

"You're away from the point again," said Macdonald with a smile. "How do you defend Janet Brown's week of anagrams?"

"It doesn't need any defence; it was Janet's fancy to play herself and I fail to see that she was wasting time. You really never waste time unless you are under coercion."

"Another rotten paradox," he laughed, "go on!"

"When I allow convention to force me to play cards I feel that I am wasting time, for I hate the blamed things. But if I spend a day pottering with the wheels of an old clock I am not wasting time: I am extremely interested all the time."

"No, no! It won't do! Janet was wasting time, and you know it, in spite of your arguing!"

"I'll tell you what's wrong with you and all your fellow educationists, Macdonald," I said. "You've got utilitarian commercial minds. You worship work and duty, and you have your eyes on monetary success all the time. You look upon bairns as a foreman mechanic looks upon workmen, and your idea of wasted time is the same as his. If I were Bruce, the linen merchant, I should certainly accuse a girl of wasting time if I caught her reading a novelette during working hours. Bruce has one definite aim—production of linen. He knows exactly what he wants to produce. You don't, and I don't. We don't know what effect puzzling out anagrams will have on Janet's mentality. We have no right to accuse her of wasting time."

"Don't tell me," he cried; "there is a difference between work and play. Janet has no more right to play during school hours than a mill-girl has to read novelettes during working hours."

"The mill-girl is a wage-slave, and I don't think that dominies should apply the ethics of wage-slavery to education. Her master, Bruce, goes golfing and fishing on working days, only, he is economically free, and he can do what he likes. And I don't suppose you will contend that tending a loom is the goal of humanity. If you want to make Janet an efficient mill-girl by all means coerce her to work in school. But, Macdonald, I have argued a score of times that education should not aim at turning out wage-slaves. If Janet is to be a mill-girl all your history and grammar won't make her tend a loom any better; so far as the loom is concerned the composing of anagrams will help her quite as much as grammar will."

When Macdonald had gone I made up my mind that I wouldn't argue about education with him again. I'll bring out my pack of cards when he next visits me.

* * * * *

I have had a sharp attack of influenza, and have been in bed for a week. When my temperature fell I commenced to read a book on political philosophy, but I had to give it up. I asked Margaret to borrow a few novels from Macdonald's school library, and I found content. I read *The Forest Lovers*, *King Solomon's Mines*, and one of Guy Boothby's Dr. Nikola stories, and was entranced.

When you are ill you become primitive; the emotional part of you is uppermost, and you weep over mawkish drivel that you would laugh at when you are well. Any snivelling parson could have persuaded me to believe that I was a sinner, had he come to my bed-side three days ago.

Luckily no snivelling parson came, but the girls came every night.

"Aw hope ye dinna dee," said Annie.

"Ye wud need an awfu' lang coffin," said Janet as she measured me with her eye.

"You've got a cheerful sort of bed-side manner, Jan," I said.

"Wud ye hae an oak coffin?" she asked.

"Couldn't afford it, Jan. You see I'm saving up for my marriage."

"But if ye need a coffin ye'll no need a wife."

"The wedding-cake will do for the funeral feast," I said hopefully. "I've ordered it."

Janet laughed.

"Eh! It wud be awfu' funny to eat weddin' cake at a burial!" she cried. "Wud'n it?"

"I don't think I would be in a position to appreciate the fun of the thing, Janet."

"Maggie wudna see muckle fun in it either," said Gladys.

"Wud Jim Jackson be yer chief mourner?" asked Ellen.

"Possibly," I said, "but don't mention the fact to him. He'll become unsettled. He's an ambitious youth, Jim, and his position as best man at my marriage will merely make him long for other worlds to conquer."

"Ye wud hae a big funeral," said Janet thoughtfully.

"We wud get a holiday that day," she added brightly.

"Ah!" I said, "that settles it, Jan. Leave me to die in peace. Let me see—this is Tuesday; if I die now that will mean Saturday for the funeral. That's no good. What do you say to my putting off the evil day till Friday? That will mean a holiday on Tuesday."

"But ye canna dee when ye want to!" she laughed.

"I can easily borrow some of Mrs. Thomson's rat poison."

"Syne ye wud be committin' sooicide," cried Annie, "and they wud bury ye at nicht, and we wudna get oor holiday."

"Ah! Annie! You've raised a difficulty. I hear Jim whistling outside. Bring him in and we'll see if he can solve the problem."

They brought Jim to my bedside. I explained the difficulty, and Jim scratched his head.

"If ye was murdered they wudna bury ye at nicht," he said after some deliberation.

"A brilliant idea, Jim, but who is to murder me?"

"Joe Simpson wud dae it . . . quick," he answered. "He has a notion o' Maggie."

"Aw wud get another holiday," he added, "when Joe was tried. Aw wud be a witness."

"So wud Aw," said Annie.

"And me too," said Janet.

"Ye wudna," said Jim with scorn, "lassies canna swear, and ye have to put yer hand on the Bible and swear when ye are a witness."

"We'll have to give up the murder idea," I said firmly: "it's unfair; I can't have Jim getting two holidays while the girls get only one."

"We micht get another holiday when Joe was buried," suggested Ellen.

"No," said Jim, "they bury a hanged man in the jile."

"Ye'll just need to get better again," said Janet.

"You'll lose your holiday in that case, Jan."

She put her arm round my neck.

"Aw was just funnin'," she said kindly, "Aw dinna want ye to dee. Aw wud greet."

"You would forget me in a week, Jan."

"Na Aw wudna," she protested. "Aw wud put flowers on yer grave ilka Sabbath, and Aw wud cut oot the verse o' pottery in the paper. Aw cut oot the verse aboot my auntie Liz."

"What was it?"

"Aw dinna mind, but it was something like this:—

"We think, when we look at yer vacant chair,
Of yer dear old face and yer grey hair,
But ye are away to the land of above
Where ye'll never more have care."

"Very nice, Jan. Now you'll better set about composing a verse for me."

"A' richt," she laughed, "we'll mak a line each, and here's the first one:—

"'He was goin' to be marrit, but he dee'd afore his time

"You mak the next line, Annie."

"'And Jim Jackson ate so muckle at the funeral that he got a sair wime.'"

"Nane o' yer lip," growled Jim.

"Come on, Gladys," I said, "third line."

"'He dee'd o' effielinza, and he'll no hae ony mair pain."

"Last line, Ellen!"

"'But in the Better Land we'll maybe meet him again.'"

"There shud be something aboot 'gone but not forgotten,'" said Jim. "When auld Rab Smith dee'd his wife had 'gone but not forgotten' in the papers . . . and the corp wasna oot o' the hoose."

"Aw've got a new frock," said Janet, and the conversation took a cheerier direction.

On the following evening Margaret came in when they were with me.

"Come on!" cried Janet, "we'll mak Maggie kiss him!" and they seized her.

"No," I said, "influenza is catching, and I don't want Margaret to be ill."

"Eh!" cried Annie, "d'ye think we believe that? Aw believe she's kissed ye a hunder times since ye was badly."

"Not a hundred, Annie," I said; "the truth is that she kissed me once; I had just taken my dose of Gregory's Mixture, and she vowed that she would never kiss me again."

"Aw wud chuck him up if Aw was you, Maggie," said Jean, "he tells far ower many lees."

"Should I?" laughed Margaret.

"Aye," cried Jean with delight, "gie him back his ring!"

Margaret drew off her ring and handed it to me, and the girls clapped their hands gleefully.

"Very good," I said resignedly, "you girls will better cancel the orders for wedding frocks. And, Jean, just look in and tell Jim Jackson not to buy a new dickie, will you?"

The girls looked at each other doubtfully.

"Ye're just funnin'," said Jean with a forced laugh.

"Funning? My dear Jean, when a girl hands back the engagement ring, do you mean to tell me she is funning?"

Children live in two lands—the land of reality and the land of make-believe. A serious look will make them jump from the one to the other. They looked at my serious face and believed that Margaret had really given me up. Then they glanced at Margaret; she laughed, and their clouded faces cleared. I knew that they would try to make me believe that they still considered I was in earnest.

"Aw'll cry in and tell Jim aboot the dickie," said Jean.

"It's a pity ye ordered the weddin' cake," said Annie.

"Ye can gie it to the Mester to christen his bairn," suggested Janet.

"It'll be ower big," said Gladys.

"Aweel," retorted Janet, "he can gie the half o't to the Mester, and maybe the other half will do for Peter Mitchell's funeral."

"What!" I cried, "is Peter dead?"

"No exactly," said Janet hopefully, "but he's badly wi' the chronic, and he'll maybe dee."

"That settles the question of the cake," I said, "but you have still to settle the question of Margaret."

"She can marry Joe Simpson," suggested Ellen.

"Aye," said Jean, "and she'll hae to work oot, and feed the three black swine. She wud be better to tak Dave Young, for he has only twa swine to feed."

"Be an auld maid, Maggie," said Janet, "and keep a cat. A man's just a fair scutter onywve . . . especially a delicate man that taks effielinza and lies in his bed. Ye'll be far better as an auld maid, Maggie. Ye'll no hae ony bairns, but bairns is just a nuisance."

"I'll be an old maid then," said Margaret.

"Now you've disposed of the cake and the lady," I said, "what is to become of me?"

"You!" said Janet. "You can be an auld bachelor and live next door to Maggie, and she'll send a laddie ower wi' a bowl o' soup when she has soup to her dinner."

"Aye," said Gladys, "and she'll wash yer sarks and mend yer socks for you."

"Sounds as if I am to have all the joys of matrimony without its sorrows," I said. "I'm afraid, Margaret, that we'll have to get married after all. The other way is too expensive: we should require to pay the rent of two houses."

"But," cried Annie, "if ye get married ye'll hae bairns to keep, and they'll cost mair than the rent o' two hooses!"

"Then in Heaven's name what am I to do?" I cried in feigned perplexity.

Janet took Margaret's hand and placed it in mine.

"Just tak Maggie," she said sweetly; "and by the time ye hae bairns Aw'll maybe be marrit mysell, and Aw'll mak my man send ye a ham when he kills the swine."

So I placed the ring on Margaret's finger and kissed her. Then I drew Janet's head down and kissed her too.

"Eh!" cried Annie, "that's no fair!"

"What do you mean?" I asked.

"Ye've kissed Jan," she laughed, "and she'll maybe tak effielinza and—and get a holiday."

Then I kissed Annie and the others three times, and they all went out laughing. The tears came into my eyes . . . but then I was weak and ill.

CHAPTER XVII.

I object to the type of man who practises practical jokes. Young Mackenzie and Jim Brown have just played a nasty one on Willie Baffers, the village lunatic. Poor Willie invented a new aeroplane; he took an old solid-tyred boneshaker bicycle and fixed feathers to the spokes. Mackenzie and Brown inspected the invention, and told Willie that his fortune was as good as made.

Next morning the post brought a letter to Willie from the Munitions Ministry, offering him four million pounds and threepence hapenny for the patent rights, and asking Willie to meet a representative at the Royal Hotel in the town. Willie rode the old bike into town, and feathered it in the hotel yard. Mackenzie with a false beard on, handed him a cheque for the four millions, and Willie ran nearly all the eight miles home to tell of his good fortune.

Macdonald told me the yarn to-night as a rich joke, but I failed to find any humour in it. It was a low-down trick.

"Good Lord!" I cried, "neither of them is much more intelligent than Willie. Any man of average ability could take them in as easily as they took in poor Baffers."

"All the same," tittered Macdonald, "the joke is funny."

"There always is something funny in idiotic things, Macdonald. If I had seen Willie's invention I should probably have roared; but the glimpse would have satisfied me. I roar at Charlie Chaplin's idiotic actions, but I wouldn't be so ready to roar at them if Charlie were really an idiot. Any fool could spend a lifetime playing jokes on village lunatics. I could write Willie a letter offering him the command on the Western front, and signing it 'Lloyd George,' but that sort of fun doesn't appeal to me."

"I'm different," said Macdonald. "I would think that a good joke. You think Jim Jackson funny, on the other hand, and I think there's nothing funny about him."

"What has he been doing now?"

"I gave them an essay on their favourite pets yesterday, and he wrote one about his pet bee and elephant."

"What did he say about them?"

"Oh, the thing was just a piece of nonsense. He said the bee's name was Polly, and—I have the thing in my desk," he said, "you can read it for yourself."

I copied the essay out to-night. Here it is:—

POLLY AND PETER.

Polly is the name of my pet bee, and Peter is my elephant. They are very friendly, Polly often sits on Peter's ear but Peter never sits on Polly's. They eat out of the same dish. Peter ate Polly by mistake one day, but she stung him on the tongue and when he opened his mouth to roar she flew out. Polly used to sleep in Peter's trunk. One night he sneezed and Polly was lying a mile away next morning.

In the summer time Polly lives in a wood house in the garden and it is called a hive and that is where she keeps the honey. I take it away when she is not looking and she thinks it is Peter that does it, at least she kicks him for it. I have told her to watch for Zeps. She sits on the roof all night watching, she is to sting the Kaiser on the nose if he comes. She is an old maid. She had a lad called Archibald, but father sat on him one night and then he swore when he tried to sit down for weeks after. Archibald died.

Peter is a nice animal and he has a thousand teeth, but Polly only has twenty. Peter looks like he has two tails he wags them both but the front one is a trunk for eating. He is an awful big eater. He says his prayers every night and I hope he will go to heaven when he dies. He had pewmonia and Polly had pendisitis, and the doctor made an operation and put in nineteen stitches. Peter works all day, the road-roller man is at the war and Peter has to roll about on the road to bruise the metal. He fills his trunk with water and wets the road first. Polly tells him when the moters are coming.

"I don't see anything funny in that," said Macdonald.

"Possibly not," I said, "but Jim's idea of fun isn't the same as yours or mine. A bairn laughs at ludicrous things: I'm sure Jim laughed when he imagined the scene where his father sat on Archibald. The essay is full of promise."

Macdonald handed me Alec Henry's book.

"That's a better essay," he said.

I read the essay.

"Its English is better," I said, "the sentences are correctly formed, but there isn't an idea in the whole essay. Anybody can describe a pet rabbit."

"That's so, but composition is meant to teach a boy to write good English."

"What's the good of writing good English if you haven't any ideas to write about?" I cried. "Every member of Parliament can write good English, but there aren't half-a-dozen men of ideas in the House. Personally, I don't care a damn how a boy writes if he shows he is not an average boy. Jim Jackson has talent: Alec Henry is a mere unimaginative cram. You encourage Henry and you sit on Jim. . . . I wish he had Archibald's power to sting you!"

"But what is his nonsense to lead to?" he said.

"We don't know. As dominies our job is to encourage Jim in his natural bent. It is enough for us that he is different from the scholarly Henry. We have a good idea of what Alec will come to; we know nothing about Jim. You have tried to fit

Jim into the Alec mould, and you have failed."

"Jim knew that you were on his side," growled Macdonald.

"I suppose he did, Macdonald. But you have got all the others; surely you don't grudge me Jim and the five girls?"

"That's all right," he said with a short laugh, "I've given up wooing them. I allow Jim to choose his own line now . . . but I'll never like the laddie."

* * * * *

I have always disliked all the pomp and circumstance of weddings. Margaret wanted a quiet wedding before a registrar but her father was eager to make a fete of the occasion, and we allowed him to have his way. Besides Jim and the girls were expecting a great day.

I can't say that I enjoyed my wedding. The bairns seemed to have lost their identity when they donned their wedding garments. Jim sat on the dickey beside the driver; there was pride in his face but his smile was gone. The occasion was too great for him. The girls stood about the dining-room in awkward attitudes, and I noted the fine English of their speech.

And Jim failed at the wedding-feast. Part of his duty was to propose the health of the bridesmaids, and when the minister called upon him for his speech he fled from the room. Peter MacMannish proposed the toast instead.

Margaret and I set off in a hired motor in the afternoon. We were going to London. When we reached the station Margaret suddenly said: "If only we could have stayed for the dance to-night!"

"Yes," I said, "the bairns will be in form to-night."

"We should really be there," continued Margaret sadly, "it's our dance you know."

"And here we are going off to a hotel among strangers, Margaret!"

Margaret clutched my arm.

"Let's go back," she said eagerly, "we'll spend the first bit of our honeymoon in the dear old bothy!"

I beckoned to a taxi-driver.

As we drove up the brae to the farm Margaret laughed.

"Do you know what I am laughing at?" she said. "I was thinking about you coming back. It's a sort of habit of yours coming back, isn't it? You don't care for me one bit; you are in love with Janet and Annie."

"Who proposed coming back, madam?"

"I did," she cried in great glee: "I noticed that you didn't seem keen on buying the tickets, and I knew you didn't want to go."

When we walked into the dining-room there was consternation. Margaret's mother went very white.

"What's wrong?" she stammered.

"Goad! They've quarrelled already!" exclaimed Peter MacMannish in a hoarse whisper.

"Did ye miss the train?" asked Janet.

"No, Jan, we missed the supper, and we made up our minds that it was too good to miss. We're going to do an original thing; we're going to dance at our own wedding."

The blacksmith struck up a waltz, and my wife and I waltzed round the room. I don't think that a wedding party was ever so jolly as ours.

The bairns escorted us to our bothy at two in the morning, and Margaret insisted on giving them a cup of tea before they went home.

Janet looked round the wee room.

"Eh, Maggie, what an awfu' place to spend yer honeymoon in!"

"Yes," said Margaret, "that's what comes of marrying a mean man. It's disgraceful, isn't it, Jan?"

"What do ye ca' it when ye stop bein' married?" asked Annie.

"A divorce," I said.

"And is there a feed at a divorce?" asked Jim with an interested expression.

"No, Jim; you are fed up before the divorce proceedings."

"Aw wud divorce him, Maggie," said Annie.

"It's difficult," laughed Margaret.

"Ye cud say he wudna gie ye a proper honeymoon," put in Gladys.

Annie sat down on my knee.

"Why did ye come back?" she asked.

"I came back to find out how you performed your duties, Annie. I'll begin with the best man. Jim Jackson, give an account of your stewardship."

"Aw had three helpin's o' the plum-duff, twa o' the apple-pie, three o' the—"

"I'm not taking an inventory of your interior furnishings," I said severely; "what I want to know is whether you performed your duties. Did you kiss the bridesmaids?"

"Eh!" gasped Janet, "he'd better try!"

"Do you mean to tell me he didn't?" I demanded.

"Aw had a broken-oot lip," said Jim apologetically, "and Aw didna want to smit onybody."

"And the bairn next door to oor hoose has the measles," he added hastily.

"And Aw lookit at a book aboot etikquette and it didna say onything aboot kissin' the bridesmaids."

"The bridesmaids didna want to kiss yer dirty moo, onywye, Jim Jackson," said Janet.

"Aw've got a better moo than Tam Rigg, onywye," said Jim cheerfully.

Janet gazed at his mouth curiously.

"Your's is bigger, onywye."

"Now, now," I said, "don't you set a newly married couple a bad example by quarrelling."

I turned to Jean.

"What did you think of the wedding, Jean?"

"Jean grat," said Gladys, "and so did Jan. What was ye greetin' aboot?"

"Aw dinna ken," said Jean simply. "Aw saw Maggie's mother greetin' so Aw just began to greet too. What was yer mother greetin' for, Maggie?"

"I don't know, Jean."

"Aw think she had the teethache," said Jim, "cos Aw heard the minister say to her to try a drap o' whiskey."

"It wasna the teethache," said Annie scornfully, "but Aw ken why she grat."

"To mak fowk think she was so fond o' Maggie that she didna want her to ging awa," suggested Gladys.

"Na it wasna," said Annie, "she maybe was thinkin' o' Maggie's auldest sister Jean that dee'd when she was saxteen."

"G'wa," cried Jim, "it's the fashion to greet at a marriage and a burial, but ye dinna greet at a christenin'."

"Why no?" asked Jean.

"Cos ye wudna be heard: the bairn greets a' the time."

Janet glanced at Margaret.

"That'll be the next party," she said brightly, "the christenin'. Did ye keep the top storey o' the cake, Maggie?"

Margaret blushed at this.

Janet seized her by the shoulders.

"Ye needna tak a reid face, for Aw ken fine that ye did keep a bit o' the cake for the christenin'. Ye'll no need to keep it long or it'll get hard!"

"Jan," cried Jean, reprovingly "ye shud na say sic things!"

"Why no? The minister said something aboot a family when he was marryin' them."

"Aye," said Jean, "but a minister's no like other fowk. If Mester Gordon says 'Hell' or 'damnation' in the pulpit it's religion, but if you say it it's just a swear."

"Aw was at the manse when the minister fell over my barrow," said Jim, "and he said 'Hell!' Was that religion or a swear?"

"Aw wud ca' it a lee," said Jean with a sniff; "only ministers and married fowk shud speak aboot bairns, and ye shud ken better, Jan."

Janet looked at me timidly.

"Did Aw do any wrong?"

"Of course you didn't, you dear silly! Jean is a wee prude. Why shouldn't you talk about bairns if you want to? The subject of bairns is the only important subject in the world, Jan, and if you find anyone who thinks the subject improper you can bet your boots that they've got a dirty mind. Jean is simply trying to follow the conventions of all the stupid grown-ups in the village."

These bairns are all innocent. When I looked at Jim's composition book the other day I read an essay with the title "The Church." Jim did not describe the church: he described an event in the church—his own marriage. He was an officer on short leave from the Front. He described the ceremony, then he went on:—"I spent my honeymoon in Edinburgh and a wire came telling me to go back to the trenches. Three weeks later I was wounded and sent home and found that my wife had had a baby."

I wrote at the end of the essay "The speeding-up methods of America are bad enough when applied to industry, but. . . ."

They are innocent souls, and already Jean is affected by the damnable conspiracy of silence. And the amusing thing is that there is nothing to be silent about.

* * * * *

The Educational Institute has sent a deputation to London to confer with the Secretary for Scotland on educational reform. The deputies dwelt on larger areas, the raising of the school age, and the raising of the salaries of the profession. Mr. Tennant answered them at length in guarded language. Part of *The Scotsman* report runs thus:—

"Asked by Mr. MacGillivray for his views on the suggestion that the school age should be raised to fifteen, the Secretary for Scotland said that, however desirable that might be in the interests of the child, it was a highly controversial proposal, upon which employers and in many cases parents, and even the State, would have a great deal to say. The expenditure involved would, he was afraid, make such a proposal prohibitive at present."

It is significant to note that he places the employers first, just as in his previous remarks on education he places trade first. . . . "People realised that if we were going to compete in the great markets of the world, in ideas, in the progress of invention, and in the general progress of mankind and civilisation, we must improve our machinery for the training and equipment of the human being."

The Educational Institute of Scotland, like the Trade Unions, is very humble in its demands. Why, in the name of heaven, ask for larger areas? Mr. Tennant rightly replied that it was news to him that the County Council is a more progressive body than the small School Board. Introduce larger areas and your village pig-dealer and shoemaker give place to your county colonel and manufacturer . . . the men who are interested in the maintenance of discipline and of wage-slavery. What the Institute should really do is to give up thinking and talking of education for this generation. The leading members come from our large city schools, and if they haven't yet realised that their damned schools are factories for turning out slaves they ought to be jolly well ashamed of themselves.

I visited a large city school a few days ago. It had nine hundred pupils, and it was four stories high. The playground was a small concrete corner; the discipline was like prison discipline; the rooms were dingy soul-destroying cages. How dare the teachers of Scotland ask that the school age be raised to fifteen when our city schools are barracks like that? I would have the age lowered to six if these prisons are to continue.

One of the delegates, Mr. Cowan, showed that he was looking at education in a broad light. "Education," he said, "if it is to be real, is bound up with the questions of housing, public health, medical treatment, and the like; . . . hence education should be in the hands of some body that would view the matter as a whole . . . viz., the County Council."

He might have added that education is primarily bound up with profiteering. Our city schools are necessarily adjuncts to our factories and our slums; the dominie is clearly the servant of the capitalist . . . and the poor devil doesn't know it. It's absolutely useless to talk of larger areas and larger salaries and larger children; the fundamental fact is that capital calls the tune, and larger areas will do as much for education as tinkering with the saddle spring of a motor-bike will do for a seized engine bearing.

Larger salaries will attract better men and women to the profession, says the Institute representative, and I ask wearily: "What difference will that make? You'll merely get honours graduates to do the profiteer's dirty work more effectively. You can't reform the schools from within. The prisons are built, and you will merely tempt your highly specialised teacher into a soul-destroying hell. The slums and the sweating will go on as usual next door; your city children will be starved and ragged and diseased as of yore."

I think it a pity that this deputation ever went to the Scots Secretary at all. Why should the teaching profession go begging favours from the State? The wise business men who rule us will smile grimly and say:—"The blighters gave themselves away when they asked for larger salaries." They won't appreciate the fact that the deputies were honest men with a real desire for a better education.

I should like to suggest to the Institute that it might have written a nice letter to Mr. Tennant. Why, bless me, I'll have a shot at composing one myself! Here goes!

"Dear Mr. Tennant,

"We aren't asking any favours this time; we are simply writing you a friendly letter telling you what we are going to do.

"Firstly, we are now beginning to make a determined attempt to take over the control of Scots Education . . . and we'll succeed even if we have to go on strike for our rights. Our Educational Institute will become the Scots Guild of Teachers . . . a sort of polite Trade Union, you know, just like the Medicine Union and the Law Union—only more so. Is that quite clear?

"Well, our Guild, when it is strong enough, will come up to town one fine morning to see the Cabinet. Our words will be something like these: 'We are the Teachers' Guild of Scotland, old dears, and we've come to tell you that we're going to run the show now.'

"Of course the Cabinet will get a shock at first. Then they will laugh and say: 'We wish you luck! By the way how do you propose to get the money?' And when we answer that we expect to get it from the State they will roar with mirth. We shall wait politely till the laugh is over, and then we shall calmly tell them our proposal . . . rather, our demand. We shall demand money from the State to carry on the whole thing. Education isn't a profiteering affair, and we must draw every penny from the people . . . just as the State does now.

"Then a member (Lloyd George in all probability) will remark: 'Yes, yes, gentlemen, but don't you see that all your demand amounts to is a change of management? You want to abolish the Education Department and substitute your President for my friend Sir John Struthers.'

"We shall shout 'No!' very very viciously at this . . . you've heard them shout 'No' when they sing 'For he's a jolly good fellow?' Well, then, we'll shout it just like that, and then we'll explain thus:—

"We aren't going in for a change of management: we are going to build a new house. We are done with grants and Form 9 B's and inspectors and Supplementary Classes for ever. We are going to spend. . . . Oh! such a lot of money. You'll be surprised when you know what we are going to do. You know Dundee? Mr. Churchill there made it famous. . . . well, Dundee, is one of the dirtiest slums in creation. At present it has lots of big grey schools. We are going to knock 'em down. After that we are going to build bonny wee schools out in the country; schools that won't hold more than a hundred pupils. There will be lovely gardens and ponds and rabbit-houses; there will be food and—.' At this stage the Cabinet will telephone for the lunacy experts.

"Do we make ourselves clear, Mr. Tennant? As you know well the State will be terribly unwilling to give us more money. If we make our schools decent places the poor profiteers will be in the soup, won't they? Our present schools do no harm; the discipline of the classroom prepares a bright lad for the discipline of the wagery shop, and, of course, a girl accustomed to the atmosphere of a city school won't object to the ventilation obtaining in the factory. When we insist on taking the kiddies to bonny wee schools the profiteer will realise with dismay that his factory and his slum-hovels will have to adapt themselves to the new attitude of the kids.

"Mind you, we quite admit that we're going to have a hell of a fight. We even go the length of saying that we may be beaten at first; for we have no economic power, and the men with the economic power will crush us if they can. Our only weapon will be the strike, but even the strike will, in a manner, be playing into the profiteers' hands; 'Geewhiz!' they'll cry, 'the teachers are on strike . . . now for cheap child labour!' Our only hope is that the citizens will realise the importance of a dominies' rebellion.

"Now, we don't want you to take this letter as a personal insult, or even as a vote of censure. You may be of opinion that Scots education is quite safe in the hands of the Secretary for Scotland, and you may imagine that we've got profiteering on the brain. We have. But we can't agree with you that education is safe in the hands of the Secretary for Scotland. Why, you might get another post to-morrow, and your colleague Runciman might step into your job. And it was only the other day that he was defending war-profits on the ground that they were forming a fund to compete with neutral trade after the war. The worst of you political fellows is that you've all got profiteering on the brain, just like us . . . only, it's a natural healthy growth in your case, while in our case it is a malignant tumour. We've got profiteering thrust upon us, so to speak; you fellows were born with it.

"Well, well, isn't this rotten weather, what?

"Best wishes to Mrs. Tennant.

"Yours sincerely,
"The Educational Institute of Scotland."

* * * * *

Jim came to the bothy last night, and his face was troubled.

"What's the matter?" I asked.

"Aw—Aw didna gie ye a marriage present," he stammered, "Aw didna hae ony money."

"The present Margaret and I want from you doesn't cost money," I said; "we want you to write a description of the wedding."

He brightened at once.

"Can Aw tell lees?" he asked eagerly.

"Please yourself," I said, and he went away cheerful.

This morning the description came by post. I think I shall make it the last entry in my diary.

* * * * *

The Marriage of Mr. Neill and Maggie Thomson.

By James Jackson, Esq., B.M. (Best Man).

They were married on Friday and I was the best man. Janet and Annie and Jean and Gladys and Ellen were the bridesmaids, but they were too many to kiss. They got a present each, a ring with diamonds in it, but I don't think the diamonds were real ones. I got a knife with four blades and a corkscrew and a file and a thing for taking things out of horses' feet, and I had a fight with Geordie Brown for saying it didn't have a pair of scissors in it and I licked him, but there was no scissors in it.

Their was a lot of people their and some of the women was crying and we got apple-pie and plum-duff for our dinner.

Maggie had a white dress on and Mr. Neill had a black soot on with tails on the coat and a big wide waistcoat but you couldn't see the end of his dickey for I looked. He had cuffs on too. I liked the plum-duff, but I liked the wedding cake best but you only got a little bit of it. The girls kept their bit to sleep on and have nice dreams but I ate mine and had dreams too but they were not nice dreams. I dreamt that an elephant was sitting on my head.

I had a ride on the dickey to fetch the people and there was a white ribbon on the whip and the horses was gray. I had to scatter the pennies and sweeties and Tommy Sword threw a bit of earth at me and I would have fought him but I didn't want to clorty my clean dickey.

The marriage seramany was not very interesting and I had to carry the ring and it was in my waistcoat pooch but I pretended to look first in my breek pooches and had to empty them on the table. I just wanted them to see my new knife.

I made a speech about the bridesmaids and I said they were all very nice girls but they are not for Janet is always fighting with me, she will make an awful wife when she is married.

The happy cupel went away in a moter for there honeymoon but they came back again at night and Geordie Brown says that it was a tinker's marriage because he did not have enough money to go in the train. Martha Findlay said that they came back because he was ashamed to take Maggie to London because she is just a farmer's daughter and I told her she was wrong because they came back because he gets a sixpenny paper sent by the post every Saturday morning and he would have had to buy one to read in the train, but I don't think she believed me, she is a jelus cat and she is just wild because Maggie has got a man.

There was a party at night and I drank seven bottles of lemonade and Frank Thomson sang a song and Peter MacMannish tried to sing a song at the same time and Mrs. Thomson told me to put the bottle at the other end of the table, they were not very good singers, Peter sang five songs after one another so Mrs. Thomson told me to put the bottle beside him again and he stopped singing. He did not sing again but he went round telling everybody that he was not drunk though nobody said he was. I always thought that he was a very stern man but I liked him at the dance.

Mr. Macdonald was there but he did not sing and he did not get a drink out of the bottle but Mrs. Thomson took him into the parlour and then she came back for the bottle. After that he was a nice man not like he is in the school, he was laughing and dancing like anything. He was in the parlour four times.

Then we sang Auld Lang Syne and Peter McMannish said he would sing it by himself just to show us that he was not drunk but he fell asleep before he got started to the first verse.

After it was finished the happy cupel went over to the bothy to there honey-moon and Martha Findlay said it made the marriage common and that anybody could have a bothy for a honeymoon, so I just said to her "Oh, aye, Martha, ye'll likely spend your own honeymoon in a bothy but you won't get an M.A. with a dickey that you canna see the end of for a man, but Margaret deserved him for she is so bonny." Martha was awful wild at me.

Geordie Brown says that the best man at the marriage has to hold the baby at the christnin but it does not say anything in the etikquette book, and I telt him he was a liar. He said it would maybe be twins and I got a black eye but he lost three teeth. I hop it will not be twins because I said I would give Geordie my knife if it was twins.

P.S.—Please do not have the twins.

THE END.

9 789361 383625

Printed by Libri Plureos GmbH in Hamburg,
Germany